ROOTS

AND

RUINS

Collection © 2025 Arcana Poetry Press
Individual Poems © Respective Authors
Cover Design: Despoina Kemeridou

ISBN: 978-1-968451-00-4

Published by Arcana Poetry Press.
P.O. Box 136 Montgomery, NY 12549
https://www.arcanapoetrypress.com

ARCANA
POETRY PRESS

ROOTS AND RUINS
POETRY ANTHOLOGY

A Collective Gathering
of 62 Diverse Poetic Voices

Edited by Jordyn Krieg

Dear Reader,

Welcome to **ROOTS AND RUINS**: a gathering of voices, confessions, questions, and quiet reckonings. These poems carry many truths expressed in a range of perspectives.

Some of what you'll find here is beautiful. Some of it is brutal. Much of it is both.

While we haven't listed specific content warnings, we want to acknowledge that many of the themes in this book may be emotionally intense or potentially triggering.

Please take care as you read. Skip what you need to. Breathe when you must. This book was not made to wound, but it doesn't flinch from the truths that shaped its authors. We trust you to navigate it in a way that honors your own well-being.

Thank you for holding space for these voices.

With gratitude,

The Editor

CONTENTS

ROOTS

AND

RUINS

Be Quiet.

Our ancestors are speaking.
We are all
the consequence
of someone else's mind.

———

TALKING TREES
Kedrianna G. Hiltonen

BORN A VISITOR

Autumn Williams

There are too many places,

and they divide themselves.

If you do not belong to one of them,

they all push you away.

The land requires

a certain amount of footsteps

added in years,

or in youth,

or in your ancestors' combined lives.

If you are born a visitor,

you might as well keep wandering.

KRADIN
Nana T. Baffour-Awuah

I was yesterday old
when I first heard my name:
a label I never loved, but tolerated;
This gift from my father,
borrowed from his second mother.

I've grown to value how it announces itself,
this big thing that demands attention,
refuses to be colonized.
This vessel of my mother's affection
reaching across the Atlantic
to bring me back
to my self
soul
name.

Kra
din.

My people believe that a name is more than a word.
It is a lamp and a map, a ship and a watchtower;
a greeting to the spirits,
a foreword to your journey.
I was yesterday old
when I first heard my name:
an appellation I never loved, an anointing I tolerated.
This gift from my father,
borrowed from his second mother.

A THOUSAND WOMEN
Jillian Stacia

It is said that a woman carries the cells, the eggs, the soul
of her granddaughter from the moment of her birth.

So many women packed into one body, one beating heart
This is science, but also magic. Still, the future is not

the only thing a woman cradles. I carry the weight
of the women who have come before me.

This is not science, merely muscle memory,
a touch of blood magic.

I hear my grandmother's laugh, I see the world through her
      through her eyes.
I am colored by her history as much as I am

mine. I am made new in their image again and again.
They are here in my heart, collecting dust among the hinges.

There are a thousand women inside me,
both past and future tense.

They bend in all this wind,
they fold in the storm of the world.

They see the wreckage before me and they do not blink –
not an eyelash out of place.

There are a thousand women inside me.
And not one of them is breaking.

WHEN THE WOMEN GATHER
Adeline Tatum

Did you know our ovaries invented

the morse code?

Pulsating and raging

ever since Eve took a bite of heaven —

that's why they hung us all in Salem.

God is when we gather.

God is when my mother whipped cream

for her flan — when my grandmother knitted

all the women in our family into a hive

with her arthritis-ridden and crackling hands.

She taught us how to grow fruit with our bodies

and would say there's a God in all of us.

BUILD A LEVEE: DAUGHTER DEAREST
AT DAYBREAK

Angela Heiser

my grandmother was cursed
marked by demon wishes
whispered at daybreak
decades upon decades ago

my mother accepted
this tainted inheritance
without knowing its ramifications
only conceding — *the women in this family are witches*

now I stand at the hopefully-end-of-this
matrilineal chain forged against our wills
sporting sandbags in both arms because
I refuse to bend like wet blades of grass

instead I fight to keep deluge and debris
from sweeping up my daughters and son
I had to, unquestionably, honor and protect
shield them from the rot-filled rage

oozing out my mother's pores
hurtling off her tongue in futile
hopes of sparing herself a reckoning
with her handed down insecurities

that mothers forget, even witches'
wee eyes and ears perceive —
children are not receptacles
for unfulfilled ambitions

and when my levee stands securely
I venture a moment's pause
toiling through the night I missed
the new day breaking and tossing

lavender across magenta-tinged cirrostratus clouds
a benediction to this next generation

POSTCARD FROM THE OLD TOWN SQUARE
Eleanor Ambler

That night,

I wandered the streets of a strange city until I heard
the sounds of my mother. Ivory notes wrapped me
in her arms; confident chords and sighing melodies rocked my
feet to a standstill among the crowd
of dreamers gathered on the cobblestones to listen.

I could not see
the strange man at his makeshift instrument through
the thick smoky haze of wistful looks
wafting around the night square. There was only

her — gentle disembodied

fingers signing thank you note after thank you note
in the ink-dyed August air, downturned
smile glistening in every teardrop of sound.

The clock's chime caught
my breath.

As I hung suspended in the ancient reverberation between

her coffee scented laugh and the

empty space of an un-chased dream

a parade of wooden martyrs filed past to present judgement on
my future. They showed me generations
of self-immolation

—   women who burn

MY TEACHER ASKS THE CLASS
TO TALK ABOUT OUR MOTHERS
Prudence Brooks

and I say mine works at the cemetery.

I tell them how I watched her heave herself
out of a grave and caught Uncle Sam
pushing her back inside of it.
I saw him stomp her gnarled knuckles
as she tried to climb out.

I am rigid at my desk as I present
my metaphorical mother
to class. I say my mom is a feral cat;
I say my mom has claws.
My mom is an anxious infant; my mom is a sly witch.
My mom ate the last Oreo.
My mom will never eat another.

My mom wrote a poem in the margins of society.
I say *She's where all my words come from.*
I say *She grew my tongue herself.*

I say none of that.

I just ask my teacher if I can go to the bathroom
and when she hands me the hall pass,
I leave my bag there, but

I don't come back.

A MOTHER IS A MIRROR
AND MINE IS A MONSTER
Valeria Eden

Girl knows what this makes her,
     what sings in her blood.
the shared whisper of hunger
that will never be sated,
will one day grow until it swallows her up.
     that penchant for anger,
the kind that spreads and rots and bruises,
handed down by generations
of white-knuckled,
     burning women.
the need to fill her body
with anything that might quiet
the empty void inside for even a moment.
the same prophetic lullaby
that only ever ends in loneliness,
or madness, or both. and perhaps
the most shameful shared secret;
that beneath the red eyes and
     knife-sharp tongue
is the same shriveled,
love-starved,   wingless thing,
desperate for the warmth of a mother.
but like all those before her,
     Girl will never admit this.
would rather bury the truth like a body,
somewhere even the worms can't reach,
until the next daughter takes her place.

would rather shatter every mirror
she could find and take on a lifetime
of cursed years and bad luck than admit weakness;
than ever face how deeply she resembles
     the woman who raised her.
she knows there is a tightrope pulled taut
between them that is too late, too painful to cross.
Girl knows that hope has wings,
and she is stuck on the ground.

BLOOD BONDS & MUSCLE MEMORY
Émilie Galindo

If only trying to   reach out

to her 'family' didn't stiffen her fingers   into twigs

—'family'   *she winces*

even the phonemes of the very word feel off;

too fluid & fluffy like foliage, too much like a fictional, flannel embrace, like a love elastic enough to reach the moon;

'relatives'   *is bark rough & like a semantic cold shoulder & viscous enough to conjure the experience —*

& wasn't physically akin to walking against

a walloping wind

with multiple muscles in spasm.

Flinching   that's her muscle memory   of them.

IF I BOUGHT MY MOTHER A DUPLEX
Merrick Sloane

No matter how the word *mother* is
uttered, it sounds severe: axed wood

ax in wood shatters a God's creation
He lumbers swinging fists & fat lip

swing a fist & slumber when
You get free; call me

call me brimstone when You bring fire
i'll be Your flint & You, Athena, wield flame

Athena, Flame, awaken to Your wield
this too can be holy: blood not just for hungry teeth

soothe holyed hunger by Your sisters: Hera,
Artemis, Hestia, Demeter where tender is not for taking

tender Your servitude for communal harvest, hunt, hearth
& enjoy Your hallowed seat at table from whence You point

You point from table & it finds itself at Your hands, hallowed
    hallowed tender
Athena, it is You tendered powerful, yet empty of wrath,
    the uncrueled God

Uncruel God, You Wrath-tender, build Yourself a hearth,
    harken Your children
in this freshly dewed sanctuary, Mother, let us starve
    hunger from fruited hands

Mother, Fresh Dew, Sanctuary, i am starved away
    from Your hands – fruitful, redeemed
no matter how uttered the word, mother, it sounds severe
    as axed wood heaved from forest

WHERE WERE YOU?
Ashlynn Delias

During the years of abuse

you were silent

condoning my pain.

...

You gently place your hand on my shoulder to say,

in the smallest of whispers,

No, dear child, you misunderstand me —

I was crying, too.

MY MATRIARCHS ARE MORTICIANS
Prudence Brooks

Tingling, meticulous fingers
weaving barbed white roses into wreaths,
dressing ancestral wounds
in lustrous pearls and pantyhose —
planning a funeral is a woman's work.

I paint my mother's pallid lips
with raspberry lacquer,
just as she clasped the opal locket
around her cousin's bluish nape in '86.
Just as my auntie swiped shadow
over my grandma's wrinkled lids
when the hordes of zealous blood cells
and perturbing memories
swarmed.

All the women in my family
have been morticians,
or corpses,   or both.

We've gazed at living monsters
and called them clement men,
held our breasts to slaughtered daughters
and deemed their wounds unsightly.

I don't want to mix blood and bleach anymore,
dusting the plums around my eyes with powder.
I'm weary of cowering inside a cherry casket
so a man can stretch out on the clean sheets.

If I have a daughter, I hope she thrives
for longer than any of the breathless dolls
before her. I hope she buries me

in nothing.

OWED TO MY FATHER
Ash Reynolds

Odd to think something

that became   me

started   in you,

a swimming half-vessel

incapable of drowning

in the   fermentation

of your loins and liver;

        my bubble breath

was your pleasure — did

you carry me   for more

than nine months? Do I

endure as hers when you

holstered me in 'Nam,

sheltered me from shellfire?

How many half-siblings

do I have with wide-legged

mothers?   Questions

were never your strong

suit, lies   your vice—

stumbling from every runny

tooth until you   submerged

me with your day's winnings;

I am receipt of your payment,

gamble;   I hope you rolled

your dice well — my snake

eyes see venom and sparks —

I am equal parts cobra

and rye. I should thank

you,   seaman,

for the import, but your

inflated freight charge

keeps me in the red.

EMAILS MY FATHER WON'T READ
Amanda D'Avino

subject: the daughter & the anthology of poems

a Microsoft Word document

is attached.

fwd: portrait of the poet with father as a ghost

the grainy facsimile

of an ocean memory.

xeroxed waves

on the custody weekends.

subject: the Georgia sky conspiring to take you

as a girl, I saw you

half-translucent.

half-elsewhere, maybe

in a different galaxy.

lifetimes later,

in the hospital bed, yellow-skinned

weak and weak and weak,

half-alive, but

sober.

subject: my mom is dead and I can't talk to you
I know, I know,   the drinking.
no need to rehash this   mess, no need to
pretend you're going to change. no matter. no
mind.   to be a father is to be a
disappearing act.   to be a father is to be a
rabid dog. gunfire. explosion. didn't you see me
shaking in the doorway?   no, you
        didn't.

NO HEADSTONE FOR YOU
Albert Baerentsen

Your faux leather shoes. Tips curled like your morality.
I still see them — lashing out beneath the table.

Your reason? Trivial. Arbitrary.
Failure shaped like a father.

I never understood.
You offered no answers. Only silence.
Threats came easier.
Death, mostly. Crushed skulls, cracked ribs.
The occasional bullet.

I was the child you never wanted.
Yet you made me. Fed me.
Watched me drown in your gaze.

You hated me until I learned how.
Thirty years: no word. No letter. No breath.

Now you lie still.
I hope the worms
get your eyes first.

As you rot,
these words will reach you
where nothing else did.
Where no priest kneels.
Where no son weeps.

YOU RUINED MY HOMELAND FOR ME
Sruthi Amalan

You mistook the first spill of my blood, stripped me bare
and beat me down until I behaved —
the way you'd beat cattle into silence.

The two of us fell into a routine:
You'd chase me into the bedroom. Close the windows.
   Lock the door.
I'd kneel before you, my knees scraping against that
   chipped Indian floor.
You'd corner me until my back was pressed so far
    into the wall
that its tessellating pattern repeated itself on my flesh,
fear stitched into the fabric of skin.

You'd make weapons
out of household furniture, turning the house into a blade.
While you butchered my body, I ingrained into memory
the beige dust floating behind your head
and the whistle of the rod as it struck my skin.

And if your mood was right, you'd invite your mother to join.
The more the merrier.
I believed my quieted tongue would make it all end faster

but it didn't.
Instead, years and years later,
I'm still there.
That nightmare, well-fed and alive,
is stored deep within the ridges of my spine.
And every time it unravels across the landscape of my body

on lonely nights,
I remember.

I remember
how you stuffed my throat with your fingers, self-hatred
  enough to keep my stomach filled,
how you treated my tongue as trading grounds, trapping me
  in the beastly hands of guilt,
how you made me regret things I never did and suffer the sins
  of past lives I've never lived,
you killed a little girl and buried her in the sand,
you ruined my homeland for me.

HEREDITARY
Raquel Dionísio Abrantes

I come from the dark hills.

Crystallized webs.

I come from the fairy groves of mistiness.

Ethereal footsteps.

I come from the forest women.

Moonlit pine.

I come from the wind of the moors.

Also, divine.

I come from ivy and stone.

Around fireside.

I come from the snakes of Medusa's hair.

Monsters abide.

SMELL OF MY CHILDHOOD
Sandra Beth Levy

I'm from hot pavements and screaming sirens.
Cigar smoking men who gambled happiness
for the thrill of displaying hubris,
their thick necks smelling of Old Spice aftershave,
leather shoes shined by Black boys in subway stations.
Mothers who stayed home to raise kids,
excited by weekly beauty parlor excursions
to dye gray stands out of their hair,
sit with curlers under sweltering helmet dryers,
blowing all hopes of freedom
too far away for them to catch.

I'm from a mother who disguised
her disgrace and poverty
when my father went to prison.
I saved my lace-fringed party socks
in a drawer, like a secret sapphire
hidden in a treasure chest.
Dragged around a *Patty Play Pal* doll,
almost as tall as me, for sidewalk strolls
on lonely days after my tricycle riding friend died
from chick pox in her brain.

I'm from a Jewish-whiskey-beer-drinking-Grandpa
who ate kosher salami and watched American baseball.
Let me cuddle him in the corner
of his gold velvet upholstered chair.

Rejected his son, my father,
but cherished me, his *Shayna Madela*,
until his death.

I'm from *Dennis the Menace, Leave it to Beaver,*
Father Knows Best, TV shows that venerated
mischievous, clever white boys, Daddy's Girls,
weak adoring suburban mothers, and fathers
who benignly solved family problems
in a charade of milk toast masculinity.

I'm from a redistricted neighborhood
where two-hundred-pound Barbara Brown threatened
to sit on my sixty-nine-pound body,
until I earned her respect
by being the fastest runner in gym class.
Where Domingo, who was fourteen in fifth grade,
called me a *Dirty Jew*.
He stuck his erect penis out a square hole
cut through the cover of his workbook
to show me what a real dick is!
Where sweet Dominican Julius walked me to school
carrying my books on his hip each morning.
Lived in a walk up railroad flat, and thought I was rich
because I lived in a tall apartment building
with an elevator, doorman, and am white.

I'm from groups of bored, unsupervised children,
who made obstacle courses in basements
out of luggage trunks, discarded chairs, and broken ladders,
to run gritty competitive races.

The big boys made little girls climb and duck
with their hands tied in twine,
pulled down their panties for a glimpse
of smooth white skin with pencil thin vagina slits,
as entry tickets to play.
Boys sang *Va-Johnny, Va-Johnny, Va-Johnny*,
approaching with glee as girls froze wide eyed,
adrenalized, hyperventilating.

I'm from a world of white privilege,
broken promises, lost dreams,
where girls were easy prey
and women carried the kind of shame
that infects your body and brain.

A world where naivete cracked open
to hatch me, a chickadee
with half a mind to hate my history,
and a beak filled with gratitude
that I survived it.

FLOOD SEASON

May Garner

My heart holds all of my firsts.
The first breath of life, the first cry cracking out of my lungs.
It holds the rupture of a dam my parents trip-wired,
so the flood has always won.

The guttural squeeze of you and sixteen,
a ruthless rise in your grip for the ripest fruit.
I was only trying to hold on.

Hold on to innocence like the sun prying
at time on the horizon just to catch a
glimpse of the moon.

My heart holds all of my firsts,
the shushed cries and soiled flesh
I did not pray for.
God crying in December's fog
as you abandoned me in winter's thaw.

You are forgetful,
but my heart remembers all.

BLACK & WHITE FAMILY, GREEN HOUSE
Rita Taste

now, no one would blink
then, questions were commonplace
bombarded with:
what are you what are you what are you
like i was a stranded alien
i never thought about how they looked,
     they were just my parents
baffled & confused when some accused me
     of feeling superior because of my light skin
if only they'd known i was envious, desperate to hide
     anything that made me too different
4A afro mixed with 3C and 3A curls, the braider
     was a godsend
i was on her porch, head cocked, hair threaded
     into cornrows every three weeks like clockwork
i have my mom's nose, we all have my dad's eyes,
     but only two of us got sunburnt
one time my skin got as red as the tint that appears
     on the top of my crown in the summertime
boys teasingly called me Alicia Keys on the 100-meter
     hurdles starting line
to this day, i come alive like a sleeper agent when i hear
     an Our Father
i can recite a rosary in my sleep
i've also sweat through hours of gospel with shouts
     of Hallelujah's, flapping fans, & stomping feet

Grandma's house was smothered biscuits, collards
    with the fixings, legendary mac & cheese
basketball ever-present on the television, framed
    Negro League photos in the attic
led to the wrestling trophies led to the volleyball
    matches led to the track meets
an unrelenting legacy of stellar athletes
Grandpa's house — skrrrrrrrrrrrrrrrrrrrrrr — record scratch —
aunts, uncles & godparents filled the gap with manicotti,
    linguine, meatballs the size of a fist
stories of butchering chickens, basil plucked
    from the garden, backyard clothing lines
    flowing with fresh linens
Midnight Mass, Seven Fishes, not knowing how to make
    meat sauce considered a sacrilege
& seriously, what are you even doing if the spoon
    isn't wooden?
what are you what are you what are you
they wanted to split me into black & white worlds
label me as lost, tragic, someone with no identity —
i will never forget when some bitch spat that ignorance
    at me
i am the stew from generations of simmering pots
    that arrived on the shores of the same place
layers of a collision of flavors that slid down
    history's ladle into my veins
the opportunity-seeking couple that landed in the Bronx
    from Bolonga traversing a new plain
the ancestors forcibly brought over in chains, who managed
    to survive and grow in an impossibly hostile terrain

such is the American way, that the question of my identity
    was brought to my attention by others
    who cannot accept duality
what are you what are you what are you

what do you mean what am i?
i am a human, i am history pronounced
the beautiful convergence of DNA
that led to the black & white family in the green house

DEMENTIA
Kassandra Vilchis

is a cough drop

falling in her mouth

cracking like the desert's lips

pockets of strawberry

seeping into the holes

of God's molars

spitting out

sugar-shackled

coats of skin

stretched over

her fingers twisting

like dirt worms

strangling the scent

of lemon blossoms

that die beneath

the tongue

a clock drips like honey

its hands dissolving

tick-tocking backwards

into the mouth

of a crab

that never learned

to swim

opens her throat

like a forgotten drawer

full of take-out menus

an argument with a ghost

and the smell of burnt toast

but no one is home

to eat it

PATSY
Miranda Rachel Deebrah

Patsy.
My grandmother's namesake sitting
   on my wooden bookshelf.
Top shelf and all where everyone can see her.

Little three-inch dolly in a shiny white dress,
Sparkles on the bodice and flouncy from the waist down.

With her matching white tiara on her head
   of faded yellow tendrils of hair
And to complete the look, a white fan in her left hand.

Fair skin dolly because back then they didn't have no
   brown dolly like us.
But she nice still.

She is part of a pair.
My grandmother has the other.

Hers, unnamed, sits on a white ledge in her bedroom
Above the small bed where I sleep when I visit,
Safe in that little house in the Guyanese countryside,

Surrounded by scents of curry and grass, unmistakable
   signs that I am home.

Home with Granny until I am not.
And am left only with

Patsy.

Little three-inch dolly
Ensuring we are tightly bound even as the ocean
   divides us.
My connection to home,
Transporting me back in my mind's eye
   until I can return.

HEIRLOOM TOMATO SANDWICHES
Brooke Gross

I was born where history never gets taught,

to a man who dug his peach-tree roots right out of the ground

and scorched the earth laden with childhood cords

so his fruits would grow golden and free.

I was meant to sow my seeds beyond

the single-stoplight borders, and sprout wings
    like the mallards

he never could bring himself to kill—blood would always

be there, and roads go both ways.

I was told heaven ran short on halos, so I

tied a yellow ribbon in my hair instead. I came back

when he called, hailed my heart to the wind,
    and made patty melts

with livermush when the homesick got hard.

I was on loan to Appalachia when I drew

the Moonshiner from a hillbilly tarot deck—
    the rare books librarian

fingered a hand-painted saw from Popcorn Sutton's kin

and said it meant I'll die young and ruined.

I was preserved where cotton once outgrew

compassion, bright bow topped with smoke from spending

too much time in Granddaddy's hand-me-down car,

kudzu curling around my ankles.

SISTER SCHEHERAZADE
Suzi Peter

I was hunched in the sun-bleached bluegrass, yes,

sifting through earthworms the color of my scabs

and cloud-crowned dandelions, scavenging for myths

to hold my blue-black sisters. They were slumped

at our foster parents' dining table, dangling

arboreal legs like tire swings. It was humid

for March, stifling as quarantine and nearly as stuffy

as heaven. Everyone was suffering funereal seclusion

but my little sisters scorched with a freakish bereavement—

I'd seen it once burning in my mother, Penelope,

my father, Othello—an unsung inferno in black, hungry eyes

fervid enough to pull us through

to America, where its sunbaked myths and bardic hills

almost could, but could not solace their primeval wound

or my ancestral melancholia, my sad forsaken sisters;

so, with a seraphic persistence, I knelt there in the garden

of incidental, ungovernable, shuddering creation,

desperate as Scheherazade, simmering with fear/fire,

laboring beneath the beams

of my little sisters' loneliness,

retranslating God.

AN EDUCATION
Shui-yin Sharon Yam

What does it say

about me & my people

that the best school I attended   was

the wet market   where I learned

what shrill deaths sound like / how tepid struggles

translate   in the body

      of a fish or a shrimp

what unfreedom   &   a slab of meat

feels like   on a cutting board

the same way I learned   to bargain

for an extra bunch

of green onions / to examine eggs

under a red lamp / to tell if an egg tart

is fresh / if the store cat was happy / if I would go home

with a playful mother   or   a blood blister poised

      to be burst

I learned silently through the   still

alive snapping turtles huddled under a net   next to

a crate of frogs — the field chickens packed   as tightly

as the actual chickens

    claws&flesh&legs&beaks   spilling

over the metal grids   the fish's gill twitched   slightly

on ice beheaded   an open cavity   still

contained a beating heart

the chunk of beef   sliced off the hook

cool and elastic   indented

with my fingertips under a rustling white delicate

plastic bag that doubled   as a shroud

LAND OF OPPORTUNITY
Sara Froi

The thing about making rice in the mountains
Is that it always seems to come out chewy
I'm not sure if it's me   or the rice
Maybe it's not enough water?
      Maybe this recipe doesn't work here

I think I grew up on mediocre food
      I just never knew it
Now everything I make
      Never seems good enough

The thing about writing poetry in the mountains
Is that the words feel chewy
It feels like everything has to be *about the mountains*
But there's the desert
      And the sun
         And the sky
And starry nights that grow brighter
      The longer you stare

The thing about baking in the mountains
Is that everything comes out flat
I just never realized
There was anything wrong   with that

Chocolate chip cookie pucks
      Crunchy buttermilk scones
Reminding us what milk and butter
      Are really for

The thing about writing in the mountains
Is that everything feels flat
When there are no light pollutants
It's easy to forget that the earth
      Still needs our protection
That this land   was once lush
      And green
Less than a hundred years ago
The lady tries to tell me
      To be grateful
That Los Angeles   stole all our water
That they changed   a landscape
Because if not for them
      We would be them
A thriving metropolis
      Overcrowded
         Land of opportunity

PHILLIS WHEATLEY'S UNSENT LETTERS TO THOMAS JEFFERSON

Daemond Arrindell

Dear Thomas,
Decorum and salutations aside, I desire to begin
Our correspondence with *how dare you*   but
Knowing well the size of the silver spoon, and the array
Of ebony you arrange around yourself,
The inevitable answer leaves the query rhetorical

Dear Thomas,
The privilege of your station confuses you, allow me
    some context
I would speak first of my birth and early years, alas,
    I do not possess them
But know that joyful foundation was stolen

Quick to paint the blame for bondage on the palms of the King
But it is you with the key to the shackles, Thomas
Your tongue is forked, forefather of freedom
So what, pray tell, could your quill have over mine?

I gift you a revision:

> *The scorn you sling at the sable race is a diabolic die*
> *Question readily the God who grants your judgmental eye*
> *This is not the book of old, in this telling you be Cain*
> *Study thy scripture that you may be refin'd and join*
>   *th' angelic train*

You think to deny what the Creator bestow'd
Religion is not my mind's originator any more
Than you can grant my freedom
Sir, I too am a child of God,
There is no creativity in imagining a god
Of your own likeness, Thomas,
Only convenience

Did you yearn to whip me when you heard word of my book?
How primitive

Your grapes are sour, your wine lacks distinction
You grant me no roots, soil packed so tightly white
    there is no space
Perhaps you should have Sally or James *assist* you

Dear Thomas,
Your quill scalpels open a surgical process
That beckons the blood you call diseased to the surface
"a m e r i c a" portraits you with independent strokes
But I know the seeds you ordered others to sow
Your words unfold like a broken treaty

While you slumber in a privileged peace, Thomas,
I rise against the morning's grief song and
Write my body a book

Let the pages turn like feathers that still fathom their purpose
Let it read like a dictionary
I will ink the words harsh as irons in dirt
But I will never grant you the dignity to touch it, Thomas

Wherever you go, carry enough water for the masses
Your name will never hunger for redemption
But your spirit waits like clams closed, missing the tide

In the centerfold I will depict a lily on the verge of bloom
Her fallen petals will reach out across the sand of your death
Let it be the oasis in a vast field of white

You have not the spine for its bounty
The pages bound will hold a prayer
For our Abel sacrifice

Thomas, you never held my freedom
I am older than scripture
I envision catacombs of hieroglyphics
Then translate them into your tongue on the page

I am not the songbird
I am the universe's wings
navigating a tightrope in a sea of snow

A WOMAN IS NOT A WHISPER

Courtney Raquelle Davis

They built the house of rights without women in it.
Then invited them in and bolted the windows.
Sojourner didn't knock.
She *arrived* — dust on her hem, history in her jaw,
stood in the middle of a room that refused her twice — once for being Black,
again for being woman —
and cracked the walls with just her voice.
"Ain't I a woman?"
Not a question —
a reckoning.
A reminder that we been here,
we bled here,
we birthed the world and still
they treat us like rumor.
When they passed the 19th Amendment,
they threw a parade for progress
and left Black women on the sidewalk.
We had to march twice.
Vote twice.
Fight twice.
Always twice.
Sometimes more.
But still we did.
With shoes too tight
and hearts too big for silence.
Because a woman is not a whisper.

She is the storm they forgot to prepare for.
She is Sojourner's echo,
Fannie's song,
Angela's stare,
my mother's tired hands
folding ballots like prayers.
We keep the receipts.
We carry the names.
We know who we are
and we are not done.

MY DEAR COUNTRY
THAT WISHES ME DEATH
Jackie Hollowell

I am born of a country that wishes me death, for you.

For you, it probably couldn't care either way.

Either way my country wants to see my body.

My country wants to see my body dead.

Demands first to see it bruised.

Demands first to see it cut away inch by inch.

They cut away our skin and complain that we are exposed.

    How dreadfully we were not raised.

How uncouth to be outside while it rains, and with nothing

    to cover up?

My skin keeps peeling, but I'm not holding the knife.

    My skin is cut away to protect you. So your skin

    can stay, intact. They would never do such a thing

    to you. For you they care either way.

I'm terribly sorry my blood has stained your blouse.

    I'm sure it is mine. I'm sure it isn't yours.

I am exceptionally certain of it.

My apologies: I have nowhere to hide such a sight.

    I've been priced out of the caves, the abandoned

    homes. I've been priced out of my own skin,

    the abandoned home. I never meant to own it

    in the first place.

My body for public consumption, my body for public debate.

My body your body the moment I decided to be born.

Or the moment I died.

Either way, it isn't your blood, just the blood for you:

My dear country.

LOTUS FLOWER FEVER
Waverly Vernon

not in this house.
not in this country.
not in that mouth.

tongue scraped raw —
bitten back, swallowed whole.
mother tongue shrivels like a cut root,
shrunk to the echo of shame.

you are lucky, she says,
lucky to be seen,
lucky to pass.

what is luck
but a cheap gold chain,
hollow inside?

what is citizenship
but a mouthful of bleach?

her daughters' scalps burn,
their skin peeled thin.
white enough, maybe,
if the light hits right.

The Airman, standing taller,
a conqueror in his own home,
pretends her name
was never hers.
pretends she was not
who she was.

even in death,
he scrapes her clean.
even in death,
he insists
she was never more
than his.

the eulogy does not speak her name.
it speaks *his* comfort.
it speaks *his* lie.
it erases her breath, her mother's hands,
her father's voice calling her home.
it buries her under a name
that never belonged to Her,
as if even in the ground
she must serve.

A MEXICAN RIVER STYX

Victoria Garcia

I would like to formally state that I was wrong.

I was piecing together a poem in my head about which body of
water I would be;
I chose the Rio Grande, the body of water closest
to my home.

I apologize for my insensitive mistake.

If I connected my sense of self to the Rio Grande, I would have
to ignore the bodies and barbed wire.

And I am unwilling to villainize the water my father used to
swim in during his childish summers.

His mother always warned him not to swim out too far, but he
would travel across, unafraid of the alligator gar and the flow
of water.

I wonder if my father was ever scared of drowning.

I know there are worse things than getting caught
in the tides.

Either way, I cannot ignore the bodies of his countrymen being
carried in the currents.

In defense of the river, I will say it's not the fault of the water
that the texas government hates the Mexican people so much,
they don't see the problem in pulling bodies off barbed wire.

The bodies of mothers carrying children, and fathers trying to
get back to their families.

I am not going to get into the legality of this process because I
honestly do not care about what is right
and wrong in the eyes of a broken system.

A stern system created to use people.

I don't want to hear about the right way.
The american way.

But I am american so if I was a river, I could never be this
river, the Rio Bravo.

I do think of her often.

I never really stopped to stare over the edge
of the Progreso international bridge at the river.

The Rio Bravo has always just been there; filled
with snapping turtles, memories, barbed wire, people.

Now when I cross the bridge, I look down
at where the brown water used to greet me
and I am met with growing greenery.

I wonder, when the river dries up, if they remove
the barbed wire. Or will they fill the husk of the river with
more fencing.

I wonder if they will find La Llorona haunting the water and
the drowned bodies of her children sunken
in the river mud; a Mexican River Styx.

Both water and woman know what it's like to cry
for lost children.

I wonder if La Llorona will finally be free,
without a body to haunt.

I would like to think the Rio Bravo used to be a happy place —
maybe it still is, in some parts.

I wonder if the river takes a little bit of people's souls.

I would like to think the memory of my father's summer still
exists in the waters.

But maybe that memory has been washed away by the
circulations, replaced by blood, tears and broken dreams.

POPPIES
Ashlynn Delias

The land bellows with
red contraband —
the victorious loot
of conquistadors
We
reemerge every year
bright red from the ground
impossible to ignore
from the front windshield of the tired Cherokee
You pose in front of opium leaves
like Sacajawea glaring back from her glass cage
We are a people–preserved and erased —
you pine for our beady, black eyes
anxious to celebrate
our yearly permittance
of taking up space
So we pass over
Our Land
with red paint

LEARNING A NEW LANGUAGE
Homa Mojadidi

When everything familiar disappears and you must leave

your mother tongue at the door —

you must endure comments in a foreign tongue

and bouts of laughter at your mispronunciations

or getting the gendered verbs of Urdu wrong; you swallow
back tears—

your eight-year-old self too proud to cry among strangers

You save the tears growing hot, burning your eyes

for when you get back home to your mother's arms

so you can pour your heart out in your mother tongue

and listen as she tells you that you must get through this

because you and she have weathered worse storms —

So, you pick up your fountain pen, the only one your teachers at your new school allow you to write with and trace

the upright lines of English, the curlicues of Urdu

written in the same script as Persian

yet sounding so different to your ears

You give it your all — to survive in this place you must learn
new rules

those of grammar and cadence and stressing the right syllables

at the right time to participate in the casual banter
of your classmates

until they accept you as one of them

'NITA'
Waverly Vernon

My grandmother said,

do not speak that language here!

Not in this house.

Not in this country.

She folded it away

like old clothes gone out of fashion,

pushed it to the back of the drawer,

let it gather dust.

She pushed syllables down the drain.

English, she said,

is the language of those who belong.

And if you do not belong,

you pretend.

So, she brightened her skin with creams,

permed her daughters into new shapes,

wrapped herself in gold;

not real, but shining enough.

She believed whiteness was a door,

and she was pressing, pressing

hands flat against its heavy wood

as if the right work,

the right dress,

the right silence

would make it open.

She powdered the truth,

smoothed it over,

made a face she could wear

without fear of being seen.

And me?

I learned silence first,

then English,

then shame.

TEXTURED LEGACY
Yomaira Cristina

My hair has always spoken louder than me,

its personality bolder, unruly, its own.

A lifetime together, yet still at odds —

never fully knowing each other.

It's like trying to relate to my mother,

her defined curls placing her

in a completely different category.

See, she wasn't taught to understand her roots.

Although she married a man with an afro,

she still looked at the texture of my ancestry

as something unfamiliar. Something to be tamed.

I was made to straighten in shame

for the pictures, for the frame.

Like our ancestors bore their fears in silence,

we escaped the pain, but not the damage.

So she'd curse my knots, like Rafael Leonidas Trujillo

cursed our history, fought them for years,

tangled in battles with my spiraling decisions.

She *still* nitpicks at every bit of frizz

that dares to question my upbringing.

I try to detangle the negative thoughts,

comb through with my fingers to ease the edges,

but no protective style could shield a head or heart

from being pulled away from its beginnings.

The scent of harmful chemicals lingers,

woven deep into the strands of my inheritance.

INTRODUCTIONS: THE KOREAN WAY
Melanie Hyo-In Han

First, consider your audience. Are they your age? If so, do a casual bow, just a quick tilt of the neck, no more than a second. Make sure to say 안녕하세요 only as your head comes back up, not before.

Are they older than you are? How much older? If they're at least five years your senior, bow at a 15 to 20-degree angle. Hold it for at least two seconds. Say 안녕하세요 in a slightly somber tone. Don't smile too much.

For those fifteen years your senior or more, bow deeper — maybe 45 degrees. Don't forget that 안녕하십니까 replaces 안녕하세요 now. Hold the bow longer — three seconds, at least. Keep your hands at your sides, your gaze lowered. Don't look directly into their eyes.

Introduce yourself with your Korean name, not your English one. Remind them that you're the daughter of Reverend Dr. 한용승. Let them know he's still doing well in Tanzania, still healthy. Ask how their family is, but don't pry. Use the correct 요 honorifics.

Don't speak unless spoken to. Don't volunteer information. When asked a question, don't hesitate.

Careful, always be careful and think about how you're being perceived.

Try your best to blend in. Just be Korean.

FAG IN TRANSLATION
Miriam Levy

Feygeleh, I see you in all the trees
little bird fairy, I hear you queer as time

We have been here since before the word faggot
wrapped itself in their mouths

a flash of yellow and a wink of the eye
swoop majestic, and balance
in this cold place
searching

for a winding staircase back, up or away
trapdoor to a treehouse sanctuary

Liten fugl, I see you everywhere

I see you in the traces between these languages
       in flytende and flyr
          fluent and *flying*

I see you in the space where English eats everything up
where nuance grows like moss: in spite,
that we could call resistance

HOW TO LOVE A HOME

Shui-yin Sharon Yam

Leave, so that you can fill it with longing
With glimmers of mundane recollections
      made precious by disappearances
With dreams, in which you utter
        in foreign tongue:
        I don't want to leave
        and/or*: The loss is immense*

If you would rather stay:
    On evenings and weekends, dream of holding hands with
lovers and kin
      whose faces you have never seen
    Fold a thousand paper cranes in a shopping mall
    Create a kaleidoscopic light show with laser pointers
    Make rainbows with a mosaic of post-its (plain white paper
will do too)
    Wrap your arms in cling wrap
    Snuff out toxic smoke with traffic cones
and wok lids
    Wear a full suit and on your lunch break, dig up bricks from
the street
      Build stone hedges
      Arrange them like so:

      ----   ----   ----

      | | | | | |

Practice fire magic
Swim through sewers
Lose an eye—and some teeth too
Bring home and feed an unnamed child
cast out for loving her home more than herself
Make a shrine, fold paper lotus for
    7x7=49 days
Wear a neon yellow vest, hoist your cane
above your head
    Use your 85-year-old body as a shield
Plunge 17 meters to the ground in a yellow raincoat
    that does not open like a parachute
Arm yourself with a boogie board or an umbrella
    see how long they can withstand:

- Expired tear gas canisters
- Rubber bullets
- Pepper balls
- Pepper spray
- Exploding bean bag rounds with lead pellets
- Batons
- Water cannons
- Bright blue caustic water
- A government that hates their people so much
  that they turn a home into
  a clamoring sea

STREET CHRONICLES
D.A. Springer

In the cracked concrete where I once stood watch,
A wildflower splits foundations like truth splits a lie.
What they call hustling — I call survival.
My ancestors knew: broken men hold the most wisdom
    in this wild.

What shatters create edges,
Edges that teach me to see in the dark.
I am my grandfather's quiet warnings,
His gold teeth gleaming like a new dawn
    between cautious smiles.

These city blocks remember me before I remade myself,
Their corners whispering beneath my tread worn shoes.
The corner store knows what others pretend not to see:
That the same hands that counted singles now sign
    contracts and checks.

I've been torn down to nothing but hunger,
Rebuilt from lessons written in surveillance cameras.
My architecture is twenty years of near misses,
A skyline of close calls reaching toward something legit.

They gentrify the blocks where I learned mathematics,
But hustle roots push through opportunity like instinct
    through time.
What's buried in my past isn't gone, it calculates
    opportunities through rhymes.
Converting street sense to business behind closed doors,
    no witnesses.

I am what survives raids and lockdowns,
What grows in concrete cracks despite the odds
    weighed down.
When the system tried to predict my failure, it forgot:
The hustler's spirit is just ambition without permission.

In abandoned projects, between broken promises,
My people find pathways invisible to others' stubborn ways.
The beauty isn't in what's clean or sanctioned,
But in how we alchemize desperation into strategy
    with no sanctions.

I am crumbling neighborhood legacies,
Reclaimed by my children's advances.
I am shattered expectations catching second chances,
Throwing possibilities across generational divides
    while jumping fences.

We are the children of broken promises,
Street economists turn systemic decay to personal gold
    commas and sense.
Our broken histories aren't weaknesses.
They're proof we've mastered games rigged against us.

Like many I am whole not because of my street education,
I've transformed pain into power through this thing
    called the Pen'demik.
Now, can I get a witness to this...

THE ANCESTRAL HOME
OF TRANSGENDER SUICIDE
Ezra Gatlin

the lost city of atlantis, known only by the sharks.
the pressure in my chest forces popped lungs to float.
my queerness lies at the bottom of an ocean;
rummaged, colonized, and eternally disturbed.

someone told me I wasn't the first.
no, my ancestors were queer.
my ancestors were afraid.
my ancestors saw the basements of the ships
and risked choking on a trident's bygone.
they had nothing but half-buried castles,
only brought up as once-great has-beens
and the slave men at the other end of bullets.

my ancestors died nameless and alone,
tongue-tied in fruitless self-preservation.

they aren't here now.
it's me who gets iced out of every wedding.
it's me who gets iced out of every funeral.
i could find community in queer if my family loved
the sinner, too.
instead, no one calls on christmas.
or on birthdays.
or graduation.

they ask in passing, to make sure i'm not dead.
my mom tells them i'm close.
she tells them about her son at home, her son in jail.
her daughter, sorry, "child," tried to kill herself
last week.

it still feels like i'm the first; a part of me can't believe it.
i still don't know how to leave,
too many ghosts made me.
these streets are full of their cemeteries.

my blood, once-removed, lies outside the VA,
just inside the shelters;
if i go, i leave the bones behind.
if i drown, take me to atlantis,
let the rage i swallowed flow the drainage pipe
with the rest of me.

if i rattle my last words into a half-naked noose,
bring me home; bones and all.

WE WERE NEVER MEANT TO BE QUIET
Courtney Raquelle Davis

Once, we were only allowed to bleed — bleed and cook, bleed and hush, bleed and bear children whose names we couldn't even sign on anything but tombstones. They told my grandmother her voice was too loud, so she bit her tongue until it tasted like rust, wore silence like a corset pulled tight until her spine forgot how to stand. But even then, we were planting things.

Sojourner stood in a room that didn't want her — black and unbothered — and asked, *ain't i a woman?* as if it wasn't already carved into the soles of her feet. We marched with blistered prayers down streets that never wanted us. When they carved the 19th Amendment into law, they didn't write our names in ink; we scratched ours in with fire.

They gave white women birth control in the '60s. We got it in back alleys under threat. Still, we took the pill and turned it into poetry. Our bodies were battlegrounds long before abortion became a debate.

Now in 2025, they still say *first woman to...* like we haven't been running this quietly for centuries. They forget Harriet rode freedom like a train through night's throat. They forget Fannie Lou cried power in a room full of cowards. They forget my mother voted with tired hands, carrying a baby on her hip and hope in her pocket.

I am not the first. I am the echo — the answered prayer of every woman silenced mid-sentence. I vote with ghosts of grandmothers pressed to my skin like shea butter. I speak with the heat of women they tried to bury.

We are daughters of women who lit matches in dark rooms and called it revolution. We are here. We are loud. And we are done asking to belong.

QUESTIONS YOU NEVER THOUGHT
TO ASK OF BLACKNESS
(FOR OBVIOUS REASONS)

Daemond Arrindell

What would be the title of your origin story?

Did you let yourself unfold all at once or did it take
a couple millennia?

How long did you marvel at your instrumentation?

How much of a spectacle was the bang?

Was that sudden influx of white intimidated by your dark
expanse?

How lonely is it to be *the* beginning?

How long did you have to wait around for the rest of existence
to show up?

What is your favorite sound to echo across
your vastness?

Is it the cicadas' thrum or the unexpected first giggle
of a child?

When did you know the handprint of your true name?

When it was peeled back the first time and the others were
revealed,

did you stutter the new pronunciations or chew them
into your gullet

before spitting them back out?

When they call you those names, how tight does the expanse
of the universe suddenly feel?

Did you know you were our god in the womb?

Did you know that birth would feel like leaving you behind?

Did you know the stories they would tell us to make you
a keepsake for our fears?

Did you know the shadows those stories cast?

Did you know the stories never stopped?

Nor did the shadows.

KALA PANI DREAMS
Miranda Rachel Deebrah

She often had dreams
of the deep water she left behind.
*Kala pani** dreams.
*Jahajee*** journey for months on end,
crossing the kala pani,
leaving one ocean behind for another.
Not knowing what would be found on the shores ahead,
longing for what remained on the shores she left.

Where is home now?

She dreams of home
has no home
heading to a new home.

Kala pani dreams.

**Kala pani*: "black water," referring to the unknown dark seas
Indentured Indians crossed to settle in European colonies to
work on plantations following the abolition of slavery
***Jahajee*: ship or shipmate

HONG / 虹

Shui-yin Sharon Yam

*"The primitive men portray the oracle 'Hong' (rainbow) as a
bridge with a two-headed dragon descending from heaven to
the earth for water."*

we are descendants of dragons
      some of us ride on Hong   gliding   through
          sites of tran/sience

     trans-:   *to cross; to move across*
                bridging; breaching

on Hong's back   rapturous with longing   we dance
with shadows   we invent
& reinvent   we break & are broken
open   sometimes gradually with
permission   sometimes
    abruptly all at once

when one head threatens
    to devour the other   I say my name
three times 任萃言   任萃言   任萃言   to call
on my ancestors   to ask:

    may my tongue stay wild?

    is freedom free if I have to exchange
        my body for the shape
           of a fawn?

    can we dwell and make love
      in perpetuity

in the liminal of the not-quite and
                                the in-between?

can I land safely home
        if I sever a head?   if so, which one?

will you forgive me
        for dreaming of your fragmented smile   but not
                your name?

my great-grandfather who rode Hong 13,631 miles
        to Cuba   says:

                        open your mouth wide   for water
                        spill into a stream   become a fountain
                        keep yourself afloat   so they could
                                be buoyant

my grandmother whom he left
        behind to ride her own
                Hong to Hong Kong   says:

        言言 lower your head
        strap yours and your mother's
                tears to your back
        build a nest   with fists full of wet dirt
                look up and catch
                        the first parakeet you see
                for the child
        who has never known hunger

my grandfather whose Hong swam   across
        three kingdoms   thrice   says:

Hong riders   are never meant
                  to be   still
            why do you think   you can
                  harness a rainbow?

my mother who was raised
            a dragon keeper says:
      I cried for 90 days when you first mounted the Hong
      Don't come home. You are not safe here.

The epigraph is excerpted from Juan Wu's "Magpies, Bridge
and Goddess: Unearthing the Hidden Symbols and
Rediscovering the Lost Goddess in Chinese Qiqiao Festival,"
published in *Comparative Women*.

WHEN THE BLACK SAINTS
COME MARCHING IN

Daemond Arrindell

Let us bow our heads
As we bless the strangers
May we bless ourselves

Bessie Colman of the open skies, patron saint
May her name be synonymous with flight
May her memory always encourage us to look up

May Claudette Colvin's *"No"* be respected
and may a seat forever be reserved
for the patron saint of refusal

John Lewis of the good trouble, patron saint
May his iron will offer us safe passage
as we cross thresholds and boundary lines

Nina Simone, Miracle of melanin, patron saint
May the mirror never blur her image,
may we all be more
vocal, fierce, and feeling good

Mistress of collateral damage, Marsha P. Johnson,
patron saint
May her name be ever a mouthful
May her likeness be ever connected with lilies

Catalyst for change, Shirley Chisholm, patron saint
May her come up be the signal for our steps forward

Sandra Bland, patron saint of the traffic stop
May her name be synonymous with not holding
your tongue
Sandra Bland of righteous turn signals,
of coded language
of being Black in the lion's den

George Floyd of the mama's boys, patron saint
protector of counterfeiting
guardian of correct change

A prayer for their true histories held hostage,
their just dues silenced with constraint
worthy of our homage and
place of honor on the altar
as we ask for their blessings
may we bless ourselves

ASH AND ANTHEM
Avril Shakira Villar

Suppose we inherit echoes. Imagine our marrow carries
the tremble of rice-fields drowned too early,
the lullabies sung in dialects the wind
has long forgotten. Assume we are made of
salt and departure — when mother braided
my hair, she wove migration into every strand,
told me that leaving is not the same
as being lost. There are ghosts
stitched into our walls, eating dust beside
our altars. I write prayers in languages
that do not know me, still hoping to
resurrect what war turned to ash. You see,
we love in ruins. My father keeps
photographs in cracked frames like
they are proof that our names once
mattered. I do not know which
soil to call sacred when my feet have
never known stillness. Our history is
a forest of burning. Each leaf
remembers a different version of
grief. Still, I water the ground. Still,
I bury the bones gently. Still, I
call the crumbling house a home.

You once told me: blood does not
forget. I believe you. Even in
decay, there is memory. Even
in the ruin, something blooms.

MACLURA POMIFERA – *A GHOST STORY*
Aspen Everett

Osage anachronism\ this love affair with phantoms\
this once savannah\ these haunted grasslands
Where are you my mastodon, my mammoth?

grazing ghosts\ eat of my allure\ this strange fruit\
falling\ an offering to you\ my seed\ seeking shadows
to spread\ this offering\ rottening

I am the evolution of ancestors without future\
forgotten seven sisters\ mere megafauna memory
my limbs reaching\ twisted trunks grasping\
my twisted figure answering

I am a living monument to loss\ a growing gravestone\
haunted by extinction\ out of time\ this Pleistocene
repeating\ epoch of exorcism\ Anthropocene blues\
this fragmented song\ so many missing singers\
the gatherers forced elsewhere\ Kansas bereft
of the tribe from whom it stole its title\
hunter and hunted\ cut from me\ bow of Osage\
sinew string\ these lands\ dressed in genocide\
in buffalo robes\ a tower of skulls

haunted by oceans\ all the pressure and silence\
all the noise and violence\ waves crashing\
land of limestone\ karstic country\ rivers of forgetting\
ancient organic matter\ man-manipulated

—a cremation millions of years in the making—

combustion engine\petroleum by-products\
becoming gasoline\ becoming oil\ becoming
pipeline\becoming polluted waters\ becoming
lost futures\becoming coal\ becoming
capital\becoming carbon emission\
becoming hole in the ozone\becoming fire
in the ocean\becoming ghost\becoming lost\
becoming haunting\\becoming burning\\

-the past fed to the fires of insatiable future-

monstrous appetite\ overconsumption\
man hunts megafauna to extinction\ accelerates loss\
ignores anachronisms\ we trees\ mourning\
this hedgerow\ this division\ this fragmentation
haunted ecos\ man as maker of ghosts

YOUR BIRTHPLACE
Zeus Fontaine

On the dark plates

Of sparrows

Of serpents

In the broad

Volcanic ribbons

In microgravity

Eons

in the bloodstreams

of Mars

Sky-blade, Earth-eagle

Hold the DNA sprawl:

Always

You are here

Always

You are here

[We lived in a house that hung in the air]

K-TOWN
alfonzo solomon kahlil

ain't no metaphor for the west side niggas
ain't no poetry past Pulaski & Division
there's a daycare with a gas station 'cross the street
they shoot
we duck
that's life
it's not about being fair
it's about surviving
a west side nigga is always on the move
a west side nigga is always making moves
take your compass back
the west side always inherits the sun
that shit was a loan
we collecting all that's ours
who to say it ain't?
we making moves
we need to move
not like a shark
like a prisoner, released
stillness is dangerous

ain't no metaphor for the west side / ain't no poetry /
we don't go to church / but we pay tithes

this ain't the Styx	this Kildare	this Kedzie
this Karlov	this Keeler	this Kedvale
this Kilbourn	this Kostner	this K-Town

my friends risk their lives every time they visit me
it's not about being fair
stillness is dangerous
i came back from NY and got stained within a month
they put a gun on my homies chest
for a 3.5
for an android
you ain't a west side nigga 'til you pay tithes
i still think about you 'Tis
how could i not?
i would get stained a hundred times
if it meant you could come back
you never gave me back my gym shorts
i never said good-bye
ain't no metaphor for death / but there is some poetry

I WAS BORN IN A CORNFIELD

Prudence Brooks

and I will die in a meadow.

My pale feet are always muddy;

my wavy hair is never combed.

I'm constantly being ordered to

clean up my language.

You can pour bleach

over my blemishes and shove soap

into my mouth, but I've got

my father's fight

and my mother's flight.

I'll disappear before you can change me.

HYSTERIA

Valeria Eden

in my sophomore year of college,
i binge eight seasons of criminal minds until my paranoia turns
rabid
and consumes me.

every male smile is a threat,
every walk across campus, a funeral procession,
every parking garage and alleyway and dark corner,
a charnel ground hungry for my spilled blood.
                no amount of light will chase it away.

my 6'3 boyfriend tells me i am overreacting,
but he doesn't have a list of dead-girl names
from every city he's ever lived in tucked into the
lining of his left lung,

                so i blow off his opinion.

i cut my hair,   dye it cotton-candy pink and blue,
start collecting tattoos like a sprouting fungus, and when my
mother tells me i am making myself less desirable
i say

      god, i hope so.

that same year, i discover i have
a stalker in my hometown.
the man wants me to be pleased by this,

you see, he worships me, he says, and
when he entered my childhood bedroom
and touched himself to the smell of my underwear,
he was as   respectful of my space   as possible.

                        i break up with the boyfriend, don't
visit home again until my mother sells the house,
        and from then on,
        whenever i hear the word *hysteria*
        applied to a woman,
        i think of the man who must have his canines still
        inside her.

HOLE
Thomas Jackson

not eggshells stepped on, a minefield of Prince Rupert's drops
step   snap   pop pop   shrapnel flesh scratch bone
God's a scream sucked back down, expelled, pulled back in

whole body tententensed fucks fly in fastened flux
cortices still undeveloped perfect time perfect time
no pause no cease no parry blame, a prison; drudge pity
all you pray for is accountability chalk it up to brain
disease pray for his truck to flip n rid a kid of his daddy

mom's face of middle fingers big man slams front door
escapes race n pace stomp feet taught what limbs are for
sis running across the street scared to get the neighbor
around in case this worsens it isn't happening to me
rattled from vicious argument, cheeks red and stinging

find manhood in broken dishes find admiration in
an unending pattern of pity to sublimate forgiveness
lights beam pulling in straight to bed, silent pray
sis runs away sleep outside her room door secret drink
myself to sleep dragging on raw knees pillow muffled
wailing who checked in on me tap tap resentment i'm

not in my right mind if i killed myself in 2018 our
last scenes were screams hand on oven glass cold
turns on emotionless no flinch as skin sears meets
good thoughts   piano songs   lineage cooking
a child is loving hugs gouge out memory in wet
cell clumps for the fire pockets of life become

steam hiss   hiss ssp play pipe organ with
breath in brain pockets walk past the blank wall
not think of the book thrown so hard at a cat it
pierced drywall paste patched red paint swiped
across match no evidence absence picking up
paint chips frantically fists punch in place
a messed-up collage as i yell *you see nothing*

GOLDEN HELICES
George Naranjo

My conflicting attributes notwithstanding,

I am, in essence, opposed to the demo of those can-doers

enabled by denominated paper trails;

clips of a bygone current affair that favors them

over the gritty gardens of the first sowers and the pruners;

in truth, I envy the inequitable bonding ties

as the greenbrier vines etch my palmar creases.

Golden ladder to the dream is byway of double helices,

but to the same effect, I feel brutally honored

to be with those gatherers up into the last lunar—

—sleeping in the caper wakings

between the cemented layers

of hard work

MY BRAIN IS A FOREST
May Garner

My brain is a forest I can't play hide and seek in.
I know all of my best hiding spots,
delved through every nook and cranny
a hundred times over.

I play marbles by the water,
the creek bed of tears,
and watch each aquamarine glass
float to the bottom; they bestow epiphora.

I poke at soft spots that never healed,
scraped knees that are still bleeding.
My life is condensed down into oak wood,
and where fallen trees lay, melancholy seeps out in thick
pools of velvet. It soaks into the moss
on the floor of my brain,
fuzzy from years of ache.

I lift at memory-logs, just to remind myself
that the axe never won.
I watch old critters crawl out from under my skin,
confused why I'm
back, each one a villain from the past.
Soil of my own kind broken back into the beds
of my nails, my hands
still lay clean, sinless.

Who buried these lies in my flower beds?
Who allowed them to grow?

THE MIRROR BETRAYS ME
Joshua Querijero

Does it matter if someone loves me?
Does it matter if I love myself?

Staring at the mirror.......It betrays me.
Is this what I really look like? But it's inverted!?!?
What do I really look like? Am I deserving
of even a quick glance,
a look back as someone passes by?
Little black sheep
                      Bah bah Bah
"Why can't you fit in?"
                      Well, I would if I could!

Always clinging onto bits and pieces of affection.
Warping it all into some kind of cursed stew.
...............Boil......Boil ......Cauldron bubble
Eat…. Eat….Then no more trouble..................etc.
A dark mixture of what once was bright and assorted.
An amalgamation of whatever I think "love" is.
A bitter aftertaste. Yet I scoop and scoop it all
into my mouth
Until I'm bursting at the seams.

                Oh, maybe I should slurp more
Since I was always told food
shouldn't go to waste.................................

Well, what else have I known but the leftovers?

Oh, if I didn't eat so much slop I'd look better
Looking in the mirror. Lifting my shirt
<u>Ehh, it's still the same.</u>
Frustrated..............I punch the mirror
Until my knuckles ooze crimson
Just to feel some kind of warmth, I guess.

Shards on the floor. Reminders of what I still look like.
At least now, I can't see myself for a little while.

FLOWER OR WEED?
Claudia Jean

My mother cuts back my rose bushes

and I feel like a child again — petals falling

before a proper bloom.

I don't tell her

how much the roses are hurting.

Instead I say,

      "they're pretty in the springtime."

Pragmatic parry,

      "they're invasive."

I pluck at my fingernail

flower bed,

and ask if the world

loves me or not.

•CULT LEADER• GETHSEMANE
Thomas Jackson

Palms to the sky, repeating the doctrine I can pull
sod carpets back and mold the damp, sopping dirt

Another recruiter puts her faith in my story
the dream career I've had since sixteen

I get to the desk it's simply empty clicks too maniacal
to make design decisions let alone life ones leave early

Written warning get COVID at a Landscaper's conference
after a combined migraine jaw spasm sinus infection

From droperidol-induced dystonia, ER to office, Office to ER
unable to speak to the clients I'm designing for
given incorrect info

Late rent emails a sports car is t-boned by a pickup truck
in the four-way intersection while on the phone
asking for funds

Parents driving hours to give cash to cover the week they
didn't pay me, keep submitting unfinished work for review

Rack up a second written warning on top of an ADA request
to work from home when the headaches get too severe

Building a paper trail to cleave me off
rather than accommodate

Leave the job leave my parents in the dark keep saying it's
going well get another job getting yelled at over the phone

By people dissatisfied with the fracture of mail-ordered
jars of raw honey from halfway across the country

Keep up the story, everything's under control
I'm the designer I went to school to become

Nothing's wrong

ONE TRUE THING
Jillian Stacia

Mother swallowed cyclones,
sucked gristle from the bone
of storm, slurped jelly

from the eye of the world's
hurricane. Savage and Starlight,
she ripped open the black hole

and got lost inside it.
The rain whipped me
awake, the swish of her hip

made men into mortals. Priests
renounced the altar, gave up
the rosary for the smell of her sweet

rosemary. Stubborn as gravity.
Spiraled as the Easter ham.
Where do I fit in?

Somewhere between the hail
and the Hail Mary's, the Bible
and the babe. Mother said

I was the one true thing.
But even I got swept up
and away.

QUESTIONING THE SKIES
Yomaira Cristina

Fifteen days after my first breath,
the heavens unleashed a tempest
and christened it David.

The storm caused massive destruction and loss of life.
My mother remembers shielding me
    from prophetic skies.

And I survived.

I grew like a weed—never anyone's first choice.
Not even my mother's.
I was not welcomed in any garden.
Tossed into oblivion, I became resilient.
They pulled and cut until grief turned silent.
I was wild, untamed, frustrating the pretty flowers,
the gardener's careful eye.

Yet I thrived.

I found my way through the odds:
the politics of underdeveloped minds.
Monsters in my bed.
Self-hate.
Doctors lost in ego trips.
Instability.
A motorcycle that drove me into a wall.

A dislocated jaw.
An amputated smile.
Friends with twisted tongues.

There is so much more in the in-between —
fractured moments that never made it to the light.
My spirit learned the feeling of struggling to live
when this body longed to die.

And although my jaw still learns to unhook its fist
and my smile endures phantom pains,
I choose myself first—fiercely   and without apology.

But sometimes I still wonder—*did* my mother shield me
from the hurricane, or strike a silent pact with David,
bartering my life to keep *herself* safe?

DEAR ME AT SIXTEEN, REGARDING OUR LEGS
Camille Lebel

The legs, smooth-shaven and kissed gold
by Mississippi sun
stretch from too-short, says mother,
white denim cut-offs.
Still smelling of Skintimate Raspberry Rain,
our legs are, in fact,
sexy, and thinking, being, embracing this word is not,
in fact, sin. The men who might stumble deserve to fall.
Pay them no mind.

Those legs are as strong as they are sexy. Good
for dancing on wet sand by firelight, for guiding a
spirited mare, for climbing into clouds and propelling
us through the glorious Mediterranean Sea. Good
for bouncing cranky babies, kicking soccer balls,
practicing pliés, crawling into blanket forts. Good
for wrapping around lovers, pulling them closer and
tangling two bodies together on cold January nights.
The legs will carry us forward, keep us upright, leap
over barriers, kick down doors, sweet girl,
sexy as hell with every step.

DEFIANT STARLET
Alecia Lewis

They tried to bury me,
failing to recognize
I was a seed.

A star who burned too brightly
for a carefully controlled galaxy.
A rebellious intellect with undeniable beauty,
zero interest in playing games and
following the rigid expectations
of an established industry.

Mesmerizing with rare authenticity,
I refused to be sculpted and molded
into a Passively Agreeable Ditz.

Refuse artificial fame.
Reject sensationalized propaganda.
This era wasn't ready for
an independent enigma
unwilling to force a grin.

Personal struggles and
intensified depression made me
an easy target for a system that
demanded control.

Discarded and incarcerated,
I endured treatments
not about healing,
but compliance.

Drowned in ice baths,
electroshock therapy,
forced sedation,
chained to a cell —

all brutal lessons in submission.

Details of my suffering
blurred over time,
shrouded in myth and rumor
with the remaining truth:

I challenged and fought authority.

I am a legend.
Not for my performances,
but for my battles.

My legacy endures
not as a warning,
but as a reminder.

I never was:
Too Wild,
or
Too Much.

I was exactly who
I was meant to be.

LIVIN' THAT NUN LIFE
Zoe Morana

I meddle in other people's affairs:
Yue Lao 月老 is about to push me down the stairs
did you know *divorce witness* is a career path in Taiwan?
homewrecking made profitable by patriarchy. whoever signs
the paper is conscripted to seven years of bad luck; most
couples hire strangers to end their marriage.
i'm a red-jacketed anomaly.
proceedings choppy. translate broken promises
from shore to shore.
"you get the kid on weekends // no the house won't be yours"
we're given a red envelope to neutralize our misfortunes, but
divorces are tough on wallets of young
russian mothers without plum blossoms
so I drop the talismanic bus money into my pockets
and shake myself
the clinking wards off the dry spell like fireworks
scare off the 年獸
but still i'm always looking over my shoulder, scared
to find no one
i blame my next 7 years of solitude on this. 籤 says: accidents
forecasted.

bad habits leave your love life stale:
on that note, i should probably stop
breaking up with people over e-mail
there's only been one tongue in my mouth this year
and it swallows books by the pirated fileful.

I drip stolen ideas from my pen tip, feel like God. starting to
suspect all fiction writers are control freaks; off-page onstage
nothing goes according to script.
that's why we love the page.
from meet-cutes to ex run-ins, many awkward accidents.

denial, cont.:
i measure my minutes by what you're doing this time
of day, each clash with you an emotional revenue
I dance through your business meetings and sip vodka while
you eat lunch
i wonder what you would say to my meddling,
you're not here so i write what's in your brain,
you wish i were calmer you wish i would refrain.
my compass still determines north by relativity to you, so I'll
take the S-bound train because our earth is round (my
ayahuasca-drinking friend disagrees, preaches
I'll fall off the edge, but I am a scientist
before I am a hippie) and if I hurl myself in the wrong direction
hard enough, I might just torpedo into you
with my ego intact, call it an accident

unmarried, currently crocheting doilies for my trousseau:
anyways, on the topic of inauspicious influences
and being cuckolded by beaus
i'm not concerned, i'm young, i've got time
only the tide and the occasional stalker
have ever screamed "be mine"

not planning to repeat my parents' marriage,
vegas drunken accident

last resort:
pick up the red envelope in the street, take my ghost bride
home to court
then i could always get an exorcism
instead of a divorce

i got options, baby

AFTER TANCREDI AND CLORINDA
Danielle Salerno

My heated flesh yields

to the thrust of your knife

I never knew how much I'd enjoy

these violent delights

So, I present my underbelly

and invite you to slice

me open with your gentle caress

Make me bleed out

From your tenderness

SHOOT LIKE YOU FUCK
Sophia Egolf

I'm on my knees for a myth,

an unfair proximity to self-slaughter.

Salivating in my eyes and a dryness in my mouth,

I'm violently devouring your grim body.

An MKA-19 and a sloppy lick on your fingers.

My hands are occupied with blessings,

death-bound

I'll take him.

THE THINGS WE'RE DOING
WOULD UPSET YOUR MOM
Allison Norwood

in my head,

your belt's already off.

it hits the ground flat —

a dead snake.

i watch acid dissolve

sunset slow on your tongue.

my palm upturned

as you trace my fate line —

tell me we have always been

in this kitchen:

a basket of clementines,

a pink kettle,

linoleum

peeled like fresh sunburn,

the cat napping in a warm slice

of sun, and you —

if she ever saw how *you*

kneel in my mind,

she'd light lavender candles

in a salt circle,

drag you to the nearest priest,

and have him hose your thoughts off

with latin

and ice water.

she always begged you

to be more devout.

now every sunday

we share a hand-rolled prayer

over breakfast

in bed.

ORIGINAL SIN
Luana Campagna

I am left there

like the core of an apple

you didn't bother to finish.

The original sin —

wanting to know me deeply,

peeling my skin.

There is some rot in me,

but that's the sign of tasty fruit.

Nature's signature

still echoing in my veins.

ON BEING FUCKED & FED
Merrick Sloane

you drop seed & I call myself soil

prepare my earth for rupture of new life
edging of root is a beckoning to come again

in the morning, you offer me breakfast
without breaking eye contact — unhurried tokens

I didn't know a gaze could be a prayer
at night, you ask me on directionless strolls

with touch whose only motive is grounding
there is purpose in the nothing of a thing

we are here; together
kitchen counter is where our hands till land:

bare feet move about unworried with time
or space as we prepare laughter-peppered meal

I open to you like a rib offered for creation
you answer in kind so we might both bloom

I am learning that a body is more than a thing
to be splayed on a slab I am learning that neck

is more than the shell that protects it
Hunger is fed from communion's hands:

grapes of tender plucked from the vine
dropped into mouths open only to succor

tongues lap up hidden innards of mind,
mine for ethos-gold to excavate and lay

brick for bridging uncombed lands
I let you graze the prairies of my body

flesh-spill sticks like anointed oil to our
waters, binds straw and sand into stir

elbows deep in new earth, we build houses of worship
elbows deep in cold clay, we bow to our adobe altars

KITCHEN GHOSTS
Danielle Salerno

I do not think of how I mourned you
before you were gone
Swallowing my resentment like wine
savoring tannins of guilt and regret
at how fiercely we loved
yet never seemed to connect
Amid the pots and pans
and maudlin remembrances
I'm embraced by the scents
of olive oil and Shalimar
which elegantly present
my grief as an hors d'oeuvre
on a pretty little cocktail napkin
for everyone's consumption but mine
The red plastic bowl
a loving container for our fingerprints
bears witness to the passage of time
marked by holidays spent kneading bread
Your ghost rising with the dough
The honeyed scent that fills my nostrils
can barely assuage
the bitterness on my tongue
but for a still present voice in my head
whispering, "Add more salt"
My tears have long dried
and have none left to provide

DL
Thomas Jackson

life is a play
put on nightly
my body, glass
prism through
which the rules
of his attraction
split from white
rays to spectrum
scared of coming
out he rarely ever
leaves his house
the act one man
swings by when
curious, runs to
women again as
guilt sets in and
by night slumps
at my dim stoop
pity begging to
use me then
deny we

LOTUS
Britt Reign

toss me aside.

hold my head underwater.

leave me to die

in the turbid water.

lying dormant to

bide my time,

I sprout new roots —

ascending beyond

the dark divine.

SHE
Elizabeth Mateer

is fully fabricated authenticity
weaponizing views for sympathy
creating a perfect victim just short enough
that you envy her bounce back
and she's off again
having more fun than you ever will
counting continents like conquests
while smiling for a selfie with

doe eyes that make men weak
and women believe
lies to the face
while she grabs you by the ideology twisting
so hard you thank her for the manipulation

She
used his emotional support
pipe cleaner in Phoenix
talk about rising from the ashes
while eating my dust
we all know this wasn't love,
it was there, convenient,
easier than keeping integrity
easier than holding sanctity
for a friend
for a fuck

She
has them lapping at her heels
like her dogs
was the validation worth it
wouldn't know leftovers
she doesn't have the taste

while keeping you at arm's length
enamored with her performative vulnerability
the definition of trauma-bonding love-bombing
wrapped in a core-powered yoga-appropriating
basic edition package

memoir written solely in
ego masturbation
so quick to satisfy
she neglected the details
her downfall being
she
can't
wait
remember gluttony is a sin

I can wait
I'll starve if needed
long enough to
Google her pen name, you'll find me
should have done it right the first time

but she's a user
so don't be surprised
when the ones tossed aside
come back for theirs

thank god
I already have mine

SUPERMARKET

Luana Campagna

You came in
hungry —
found my heart
in the fresh produce.

Squeezed me
like ripe fruit.
Spat out the bruises,
kept the sweet.

Asked for love
like it was two-for-one.

Questioned the return policy
when my pain
didn't taste like comfort.

Still, you search the aisles
for a price tag
on something
you are meant
to grow.

CONVERSATIONS WITH MY PRIESTS AT MY CATHOLIC ELEMENTARY SCHOOL

Ash Reynolds

"What did Eve do wrong?"
"She gave into temptation."

> He told me her evil lived in me too.
> I thought about how I made my girl Barbies
> fuck; surely that'll send me to the snake pit.
> According to scripture, I was born this way —
> Original Sin nourished me.

"Is God a man or a woman?"
"Yes," he replied. "Both —
and neither."   I was 8,

> building my first memory of home.
> Memorizing the layout: here and there
> are the same place if you fold the map.
> Gender is a wormhole.

"Was Mary a virgin forever?"
"She was God's."   (I think that means yes.)

> I remember thinking, how dreadful
> to be known for what you never had.
> Indigo ink: the sign of the cross
> painted on my vulva
> Father, Son, and Holy Hymen.

Strange intimacies, these conversations —

> like baptism-water through my hair
> or the slice of a Bible papercut.
> Their words haunt my sulci, seeping
> into crevices only god knows about,
> or at least, that's what I let them think.
> I reign supreme; this poem is a mirage.

THE BAPTIST'S LEGACY
Jay Rafferty

There were ten
of us at Golgotha
when my nephew
was baptized.
The fount was under
station thirteen and
the water had been
heated for the baby.

St. John would have
had forty done in that
time says I to Father T.
Dunk, toss, dunk, toss.
Locusts and honey do
not make one gentle nor
jaded, just efficient.

Get ye from the Jordan,
that's miles from Golgotha
and nowhere near a station
of the locomotive or artistic
relief kind. The Baptist, head
-less, will still be at work
though there's no one
lining up to be cleansed.

HYMN WITH DIRTY HANDS
Allison Norwood

church taught me nothing.
god is so precise —
wants it all done a certain way:
dress, sit, worship,
sing, marry, fuck.
his way.
and i tried.

my feet rebelled first,
against the smooth plankiness
of the floors between pews.
they ached
for the rough, textured bark
beneath them crossing creeks.

i never learned the clean
sort of worship —
palms upturned,
satin gloves,
sunday shoes.

my hands peeled themselves apart,
reaching instead
for long-fingered branches
and sun-ripened berries —

grown in secret spots
only birds know of.

mine is the gospel
of trailer park gravel,
knees in the mud,
prayer through a bitten lip,
through a cigarette burn.
hands stained
with mulberry juice,
motor oil,
mascara.

i have loved
with both fists buried
in the earth,
fingernails black as confession.

god never came to me
in any chapel —
but once,
in a field behind the old church,
where the wild mint grows,
i spoke to her
with dirt in my mouth.

POEM FOR THE WOMAN
I DID NOT BECOME
Prudence Brooks

You are beautiful and you are not me.

Mahogany hair brushing against your butt,
bible nesting on your nightstand,
you hang your husband's work pants on the line,
pretend you aren't weary of waiting for the sun to show.
Act like you aren't avoiding your own coming out day.
I promise I won't tell on you.
We're both good at keeping secrets.

We know how to hold the impossibly heavy,
how to push a dead car across a merciless desert,
how to tune out a shrieking siren.
We are two sides of a Catholic coin,
the one who stays and the one who escapes.
You, a stale communion cracker
trapped beneath a man's stiff tongue.
Me, a hunk of bakery bread slathered
in real butter and still warm.

Aren't you grateful only one of us is real?

FOR WHEN THE FAIRYTALES LIE
Tyler R. Harris

10. Pretend as though there is nothing more you want
    than to be alone.
        oh no that was my plan all along thank you
        for inquiring dude at the bus stop!
No one wants to hear you blubber about your sad life tuck it
away   a cyanide pill in a molar.

9. Brush the comments off like cobwebs cluttering a corner.
    "you blind loser, you're obviously a virgin"

8. Smile around the fist in your mouth
    hope your face stays like that
        you're too pretty to frown, show me a smile bitch
curl back your lips expose the graveyard behind them.

7. Build a fortress of pillows and blankets, eat a pint
    of mint-chocolate ice cream.

6. Fake laugh harder than those orgasms
        thank you for asking about my impending
        lonely demise, woman in The Gap
this emptiness in my crooked grin is done with smoke
    and mirrors
illusions   delusional girls still believing the fairytales.

5. Where is this prince you're waiting in your tower for?

4. Remind yourself that nothing is wrong with you
    despite blue coroner bags under your eyes
purple vines snaking up your wrists like ivy
open wounds like gaping bloody mouths scattering
        your pale thighs.

3. Keep your eyes closed so no one sees the action
    movie explosions behind them.
        Focus on your breath   in out in
gasoline in your gut waiting for their matchstick mouths.

2. Stop making excuses
    the suicide note you keep under your mattress
    like a secret porno mag
        won't be the answer to the question on the test.

1. Never believe what they say
            the boy with eyes like cat's eye marbles,
            promising not to leave
your thoughts like entrails spilling out onto the tile
in your mother's kitchen.

They never told you the prince charmings aren't real,
the big bad wolf is.

DARE

Eleanor Ambler

All of these poems have been about death.

Curious, how much easier it is to write sepulchral scriptures
than to capture

the complexities of life. There are rays of light
on everything we see,

but darkness draws eyes with her mysteries
and even the moon, in all her

distant splendor cannot compete with the unknown infinity of
the

night sky. I promised once to bear witness to the world's
beauty.

My promise was swallowed in corners and cobwebs,
in dusks

after sunsets, in shadows under curves of bodies and in

orifices, opening into undefined landscapes. It is simpler

to slide silently into sleep than to stare at the sun.
It is safer to slip

into solitude than to try to decipher a smile. I dare you, world,
to show me

your teeth. Spring is coming. I will watch the flowers bloom.

LAST WILL & TESTAMENT TO THE UNIVERSE
Taylor Andresen

Consider this my last will and testament to the universe; instructions for how I wish to be regenerated, alchemized, and given intentionally like a family heirloom to whoever needs to be haunted by my love the most.

First, place the pulse of my heartbeat into the mandolin of a 20-year-old lesbian serenading her soulmate in front of her libertarian dad and Christian mom at a college glee club show.

Breathe the air from my lungs into every book I've annotated in our library of a living room. Notice the network of my neuropathways left behind in notations in novels and neuroscience textbooks.

Place a piece of my soul in the ink of a pen held in the shaking, arthritic hands of an 86-year-old woman as she shades in her vote for the first woman elected president without telling her husband what she's done. And this time we win.

Emit the electric charge from my existence's vibrational frequency to power the speakers connected to a microphone held in the hands of a spoken word poet as they speak the truth of what happened to them with such force that it exorcises all of the self-doubt and cell deep trauma from their deepest somatic center. Give them the liberation they always deserved as their reality is finally witnessed and reflected back to them with a fiercely firm certainty by a community of strangers in a random bar on Roy Street.

Let my moon brother find me in the clouds of bong rips. Moon boy, whether you like it or not, I'll send my voice through the bubbling bong water to lecture you for the hundredth time to stop settling for women with overhead light energy who don't see the magic in your messiness; the kindness amidst your chaos; the love in your lunacy. Keep looking for the girl who sees every burst of anxiety as a chance to sync her breathing with yours; knowing that the gift of that kind of connection could never be a burden.

My wife already knows to look for me in every piece of lavender, in every fire pit ember, in every out of place Third Eye Blind and Counting Crows song playing in a public space. I told her where I'll be so that not even over my dead body will she ever feel alone.

MIDSUMMER SPELL

Jessica Aure Pratt

Women and femmes dressed as fairies,

as fire, the sun, the audacity,

at the wool waulking table,

singing Scottish folk songs,

in the woods, becoming new,

in the river, skinny dipping,

at the feast, tasting wine,

at the campfire, drinking starlight,

at the maypole, twirling to Chappell Roan,

Morris dancing, handkerchief in hand,

bells on ankles, tinkling to Små Grodorna,

reading Mary Oliver, reciting Joy Sullivan,

reading Norse myths, delighting in tea and chocolate,

divination by candlelight, perusing runes and decks,

levity and wonder washing us with moonlight.

Don't let anyone tell you magic isn't real.

I have devoured it whole.

PULLING THE 9 OF PENTACLES ON A HUNGRY DAY

Ash Reynolds

Snakes nest in my ventricles:
slithering subtle sickles
move in, lay eggs
in my lungs—breath transforms
into mud pies in my mouth.
I draw a tarot card for my future:
a feast for my divine electricity —
there is a heartbeat in all I consume;
I am sitting down at a long table,
dusting my fingertips over the knots.
I am eating my own flesh
and it is making me full.
The tarot card speaks fixed:
I am not a witch,
I am a scavenger.
I am a screwdriver.
I am a spectacle.
I am the antidote to plentitude,
the anecdote of hunger.

SAMHAIN AT RÊVER

Shelby Cohen

The veil is thin.
The grey sky drips.
The heavens eclipse to show their dominion.
The Halfhaven beckons, its skeletal branches stark in the fog,
    russet leaves swirling slow demise.
We revel in our macabre attire, feasting on devil's food.
We dance a ghastly pas de deux in fire-lit circles
    'round the floor.
We whisper, at the close:
May the candle go unlit.

A benediction. A ward.
A litany to the darkness, to spare a lone soul.
The spectral anguish of one long ago doom us all to this curse.
It stalks us, unflagging, as decades slip past.

Taking one from each lifetime, its clutches unmatched.
We gather once more, in sinister halls, to mourn and beseech.
To escape the malediction of the flame of Marie.
May the candle go unlit.

For if the flame finds you, on a day dark and grim.
Your dream turns to nightmare, your riches forfeit.
Death's dogged tentacle creeps across icy shores, and the curse
    of Rêver falls upon thee.
Why must we light tapers?
Why must we kindle hearths?
The flame is our enemy, our killer, our bane.
But gather, we must and say again:
May the candle go unlit.

DEMETER AND PERSEPHONE
Jillian Stacia

You would snuff out the sun,
smother her with your skirt.
Claw at the Earth
until the dirt
under your nails
smelled of death.
Your wail would swallow
each and every world.

      Mother,
      you are my mythology.
      Your stories are sewn
      into my bones, holding me
      together like stitches.
      You care nothing of fate.
      You'd let it all fall
      to ruins.

Mother, of this I have no doubt —
                you'd stop the seasons for me.

ORACLE
Jessica Aure Pratt

A full dewy moon drips waxy
beams, teacups steaming out
galaxies in a candlelit room,
new friends in a circle.

I ask for a reading, a deck
and a question in hand.

Lauren says *I don't think you're*
asking what you really want
to ask, your question is too nice.
What are you actually trying to get at?

I recognize I've been protecting myself —
the question underneath is much
tougher to chew on, to spit out.

I peel back the protective coating,
sticky and vulnerable,
ask anew, vitals bare.

I begin to understand —
women are the diviners,
the deck is poetry.

WE HOLD THE OXYMORON
OF DOUBT AND CONVICTION

Noel Aquino

this irony exists in all of us,
like sewage speaks decay,
yet water still remains—storied,
filtered through scars, marks, muck, and stars,
I ponder… what is it to live
if we merely drift to our destined passing?
maybe we're moving, like night and day,
part of the earth's ceaseless cycling?

then perhaps we're of the night sky—
the universe's window to the past,
God's eternal river,
His educating arm,
bidding us to look beyond the easy,
to witness the scale of our history—
in the confusing chaos
is a harmonic beauty,
in the darkness of the cosmos
lies a smooth synchronicity—
saying we are still in the present,
yet always forward moving—
to cherish our moments,
for we aren't meant to last.

and despite limitations,
we shrink the unknown,

chasing new discoveries,
blessed with eyes of curiosity—
looking past the foul smell of septic,
watching life shimmer through the murk,
zooming into the void of space,
watching stars pierce through the dark—
finding lessons to be learned,
even in the blackness and filth,
like creation stirs
even in the silt.

in the old days, we'd ignorantly say
this is magic.
now I look around and find us all—
oddly epic...

CROW CLAN SISTER
Avis Blackbird

Tell me your Northern stories

The sunless days filled with light

Show me the grand matriarchs we might one day become

Stoic beauty forged like sinew

Let me tell you about our Indian Cowboys

Let me share the stories from the place of suns and moons

Our ancestors lived a good day today

They laughed and celebrated with us Crow sister

MY FAVORITE PART
Nicole Avila

Oh, girl,

If you're reading this,   you've made it,

through the rubble   and the rain.

And I know   your honeysuckle lips   will twist
with slight reservation

to fight back   both the smile   and the smell
of the flowers you deserve to savor.

And I know   your calloused hands   are hiding
beneath the soil of the rock bottom
you've climbed out of,

pulling up the roots   of revenge   that've infested
your family tree.

As you nestle   in the muddy middle,
of the aphids that eat away at your joy,

find an insatiable appetite for pests,
aside from those you've grown immunity from,
who live as weeds of worship to your worthiness.

You are worthy   of the fresh breath of air
that whistles in the wind,

A rebellion   for all the times   it was stale,   and old,
and familiar.

You are worthy   of a community of companions,
                    planted in your orbit,

to make gravity feel more like grounding
                              and less like drowning
beneath the excess water of the rain,   of the sorrow,
                    of the pain.

You are worthy   of the warmth   of the fire   that burns
                    within your heart.
A furnace   for remembering   not to forget yourself,
               just to become someone else
                         they might prefer to grow around.
Instead go around,   and rise against
                              the rage of their rhetoric.

You are   a worthy reason   to resist.

THE ANCESTOR
Jessica Aure Pratt

I contain multitudes:

eons of gravity and stardust,

primordial soup,

creation myths,

firelit caves and bubonic plagues,

polygamous prophets,

and mayflower colonists;

heartbreak and longing

and a scream for survival

stretching out through time.

I am:

an eventuality,

an improbability,

the culmination of it all,

somewhere in the middle of it all,

maybe just the beginning.

ACKNOWLEDGEMENTS

First and foremost, thank you to the poets who shared their work with this anthology. Your words brought this book to life, and we're honored to hold space for your stories on these pages.

To everyone who submitted (whether your poems found a home here or not), thank you. Your vulnerability, craft, and vision inspired us throughout the selection process, and your presence in the community matters deeply.

To our early readers and beta editors (you know who you are), your thoughtful feedback helped shape this book with clarity and care.

To the readers and supporters of Arcana Poetry Press, thank you for believing in independent publishing, in poetry, and in the value of these voices. Your support helps make books like this possible.

Finally, on a personal note: editing this anthology has been both a privilege and a responsibility. Curating this collection meant listening closely to the truths entrusted to us. I hope this book meets you wherever you are at and offers something honest in return.

With gratitude always,

Jordyn Krieg (she/her) | *Founder, Editor*
Arcana Poetry Press

ABOUT THE POETS

Raquel Dionísio Abrantes (she/her) is a Portuguese poet. She has a Bachelor's Degree and a Master's Degree in Cinema from the Universidade da Beira Interior. Raquel gave a Master Class in Writing of Scripts about Narrative Structure. Her writing has been published by literary journals and magazines. Find her on Instagram @poets_desk.

Sruthi Amalan (pen name: Cypher, pronouns: she/her) is a self-taught brown and queer Tamil diaspora poet living in Canada. Her work has been featured by the Ontario Poetry Society and is set to appear in the Canadian Syncopation Literary Journal, Queer Gaze Mag and Apricot Press. Sruthi has many interests besides writing, including reading, drawing, and creating graphic designs. In her spare time, she loves to watch local music and theatre performances, spend time with her father and brother, and play board games with her friends. Sruthi released her first poetry chapbook, 'Where the Clay Meets the Flame,' in February 2024. Find her on Instagram @sruthi_amalan_0.

Eleanor Ambler (she/her) is a poet and professional dancer originally from Massachusetts and currently based in Illinois. She is the author of one chapbook "Ballet is my Boyfriend" (Bottlecap Press, 2022). Her poetry has been featured in anthologies from Querencia Press and Nymeria Publishing, as well as in literary magazines including The Foundationalist and LUX Creative Review. Ambler's writing has been commissioned as part of musical scores for choreographic works by the Rhode Island based Choreography Project (2021) and by Ballet Quad Cities (2023). Ambler holds a B.S. in Sociology and a B.A. in English from Arizona State University. Find her on Instagram @snorabel49.

Taylor Andresen (she/they) is a Seattle-based poet, wife, musician and psychotherapist. She writes of dykes, disease, and the depths of unconditional love. Her work is influenced by her lived experience as a queer, disabled survivor. Her poetry exists as a legacy of lessons on how to love well while dying. They work as a LMHC in community mental health primarily serving the LGBTQ+ community and mentoring the next generation of queer therapists. She can often be found in the woods listening to divorced dad rock while reading Audre Lorde and writing love poems for her chosen family. Find them on Instagram @casandtay.

Noel Aquino (he/him) is a FilAm poet who strives to write the same poem in two languages. He began his journey in the Philippines, and now calls Houston, Texas his home. He enjoys reading and writing poems that use heavy imagery, a usual callback to his visual orientation, and is the author of the poetry collection *This Adobo Life*. His hobbies include watching anime and movies, playing board games and video games, and hiking or camping to disconnect and unwind. Find him on Instagram @imandq.

Daemond Arrindell (he/him) is a multi-genre writer, film maker, educator, performer, and equity consultant of Black and West Indian descent. He is interested in found poems, visual poetics, persona, experimentation and exploring what legacy means. His work has appeared in *City Arts, Specter, Crosscut, Poetry NorthWest, Seattle Review of Books* and *The Pitkin Review*. Daemond earned an MFA in Creative Writing from Goddard College and is seeking publication for his manuscript "*In Search of the Drapetomaniacs*." He lives, writes, and teaches in New York City. Find him on Instagram @daemondarrindell

Nicole Avila (she/her) is the author of *Brainwaves: A Symphony of Frequencies*. As a mother, educator, and lover of poetic justice, she understands what a privilege it is to use your voice and even more so, to have a platform for it. At her core, she's just a Midwest girl living in a West Coast World. She has been writing since she learned to use poetry as rebellion against the formulaic writing she often felt reduced by growing up. She is a fellow of the San Diego Area Writing Project, an advocate for inclusive classrooms, and a coach for young writers. Find her on Instagram @nikkitine36.

Albert Baerentsen (he/him) writes about silence, inheritance, and the ghosts we carry under our skin. His work explores the brutal intimacy of family trauma, displacement, and unspoken grief. He believes poetry should wound, not weep — and that truth, when sharpened, can cut through lineage. Born in 1972, he lives in Switzerland and often wakes before dawn. He is currently working on a psychological novel about survival, memory, and systemic violence. When asked why he writes, he replies: because forgetting is too easy, and forgiveness too often is a lie. Find him on Instagram @albert_baerentsen.

Nana T. Baffour-Awuah (he/him) is a Ghanaian writer currently based in New York. His writings have been published by Hudson Valley Writers Guild, The Universes Poetry Journal, The Poetry Lighthouse, African Writer, HuffPost, The Good Men Project, and more. Nana is fascinated by the human condition, and he uses his writing as a tool to examine, reveal, and make meaning of it. He is a proud graduate of Vassar College. Find him on Instagram @whatnanawrote.

Avis Blackbird (she/her) is an author, poet, visual artist and photographer. She is a member of the Indigenous Arts Collective of Canada, holds bachelor's and master's degrees from UBC and is currently completing her graduate work for counselling. Avis Blackbird's full-length poetry book will be released in 2026 through Brick Books Publishing. Find her on Instagram @avisblackbird.

Prudence Brooks (she/her) is a poet raised in rural Indiana, now residing in Portland, Oregon. She is the author of the poetry collections TRUCE and SAVED. Her work has appeared in Pile Press, Feral Journal of Poetry and Art, Eunoia Review, Querencia Press, Black Fox Literary Magazine, Grey Coven Publishing, and others. Find Prudence on Substack (@prudencebrooks), Instagram (@prudence.writes), or look for her on Patreon (Prudence Brooks).

Luana Campagna (she/her) is an Italian writer who weaves poetry and short stories in both Italian and English. Her work explores memory, identity, and the quiet moments that shape us. With roots in Italy and a heart shaped by many places, her words capture the in-between spaces of life—what is said, what is felt, and what is left behind. Find her on Instagram @anotherhumanstory.

Shelby Cohen (she/her) is a writer whose poetry can be found in Beneath the Garden, Witches Magazine, Rundelania, and Anomaly Poetry's Rituals 2025 anthology. Her fiction has been published in All Worlds Wayfarer and Suburban Witchcraft literary magazines, and Grey Coven Publishing's Shadow Work: Volume 2. She lives in Upstate New York and is nearly through drafting her third novel, sitting at her kitchen table. Find her on Instagram @thebaronessshelby.

Yomaira Cristina (she/her) is an indie poet living in Arizona. Her poetry, rooted in lived experience, examines what heals, what haunts, and what survives. She is the author of *Luna Moth After Midnight (2025), Verses of Self-Reunion* (2024), and *This Is How I Forgive Myself* (Bottlecap Press, 2023). Her poetry has appeared in *World Legends and Stories: The Sun and the Moon* (2024). Yomaira's work also extends into a small business offering products inspired by her writing and rooted in expression and empowerment. Find her on Instagram @yomaira.writes.

Amanda D'Avino (she/her) grew up under the Florida sun but currently resides by the sea on the south coast of England where things feel just gloomy enough. She enjoys poems that sit somewhere between tenderness and discomfort. She loves her dog, Sunday, her husband, awkward silences, and the beauty in things that don't quite fit. Find her on Instagram @fleurals.

Courtney Raquelle Davis (she/her) is a poet and educator from Palm Beach County, Florida. Her debut poetry book, r*oots and roses*, explores themes of love, loss, resilience, and identity through vivid storytelling and powerful imagery. With over a decade of experience shaping young minds, Courtney writes to uplift and represent women of color. She holds a degree in English and is a member of the Academy of American Poets. Through her work, she invites readers to find strength in vulnerability and beauty in healing. Find her on Instagram @_royalcourt.

Miranda Rachel Deebrah (she/her) is a Guyanese-born writer, actor, and performance artist who combines art and activism to increase meaningful representation and visibility for the Indo-Caribbean diaspora, infusing her native Creolese dialect within her creations. She has starred in various original South Asian/Indo-Caribbean stage productions in NYC and appeared in the documentary film "Double Diaspora: A Portrait of Indo-Caribbeans in New York." Her poetry is featured in the new groundbreaking anthology *I Will Not Go: Translations, Transformations, and Chutney Fractals*. Miranda also works as a clinical psychotherapist for people of all ages in New York City, centering intergenerational healing and liberatory practices. Find her on Instagram @mira_baii.

Ashlynn Delias (she/her) is the author of *Sana Sana* and *Beauty and Ashes*, with writing featured in publications like *Her Campus* and *Williamson County Sun*. Born and raised in McAllen, TX, Ashlynn explores themes of faith, identity, and cultural heritage through a Latina lens—often with a dash of humor and a whole lot of heart. While her work has earned awards in the field of religion scholarship, she's most passionate about connecting with readers and collaborators on a personal level. Whether she's writing, reflecting, or just laughing through life, Ashlynn believes in the power of story to heal, challenge, and bring people together. Find her on Instagram @scrawledinashes.

Valeria Eden (she/her) is a writer, editor, and circus enthusiast living in Colorado. She has a BA in Psychology from Boston University and an MFA from Naropa University. She is the author of *Tender Teeth* (Jack Wild Publishing) and loves to write about the things that haunt her. She has three dogs, two therapists, one boyfriend, and her favorite color is green. Find her on Instagram @poetvaleriaeden.

Sophia Egolf (she/her) is a recent psychology graduate from Georgia State University and is based in Atlanta. Sophia's work would hope to be described as "an eerily beautiful door only women can open." Sophia hopes to continue pushing her writing out from the dungeons of her notes app, and into spaces where people can hold and sit with it. Sophia hopes to open a bookstore/cafe within the next few years, so she can build community in her love of reading and writing. Find her on Instagram @sophia_egolf.

Aspen Everett (they/him) is haunted by the casualties of modernity. Creating what they call *Heathen Mythology*, Aspen hopes to return readers to reverence for the More-than-Human by creating myths of mutualism. Aspen is the author of *Tributaries*, available from Middle Creek Publishing, an instructor with Lighthouse Writers of Denver, and chair of Geopoetics with Beyond Academia Free Skool. They live in Boulder, Colorado with their sixteen-year-old, beneath the shadow of Mt. Arapaho. Find them on Instagram @aspengrovepoetry.

Zeus Fontaine (they/them) is a multimedia artist and writer living and working in Brooklyn, New York. Born in London to Iraqi and Polish parents, they have self-produced four works of experimental poetry: *In the Land of Birds and Serpents, Splayed Loop/Gridded Vortex, A Smiling CGI God Stands Before You*, and *Above All Lands/Under All Skies*. Their work has appeared in Homesick's Intifada issue and on restroom walls in bars across Brooklyn. Find them on Instagram @jade_fugazi.

Sara Froi (she/they) is a poet who grew up in the rural Sierra Nevada mountains. She writes about the crushing weight of capitalism, climate change, and leaving the faith of her parents. She's been a featured performer at Poets Underground in San Diego, UnPoetry in Seattle, and Speak Out in Seattle. She's had poems published places such as the San Diego Poetry Annual, Poets Underground Anthology, and Ambrosia. Find her on Instagram @sarafroi.

Émilie Galindo (she/her) felt that subtext & symbols loomed over her childhood. As she watched her family trip over their own patterns, she couldn't help but become wary of what she loved most: storytelling (and its pretty patterns). That's why her writing aims to question the myriads of surrealistic motifs, motives & mementos stowed away in our anecdotes or homespun narratives. Her debut novella *Acid Taste: Excavating the Homesick's Blues* is out thanks to the wonderful support of Querencia Press. Find her on Instagram @wildthingxumakeverythingroovy.

Victoria Garcia (she/her) is a current MFA poetry candidate at Texas State University. As someone from a border town, she writes about her identity as a Mexican-American from an immigrant family. Her poetry can be found in Cuentame Literary Magazine, Livina Press, and Apricity Press. Find her on Instagram @victoria23garc.

May Garner (she/her) is a poet and author based out of Dayton, Ohio. She has been crafting and sharing her work online for over a decade. She is the author of two poetry collections, *Withered Rising & Melancholic Muse*. Find her on Instagram @crimson.hands.

Ezra Gatlin (any pronouns) is a black, transmasculine poet from Aurora, Colorado. They have several forthcoming publications, most recently including Vellichor Literary, Whispering Fields Review, and Femme Dyke Zine. They made their gallery debut in April 2025 with the RISE 2025 Art Show in Denver. Find them on Instagram @bloodbornepoetry.

Brooke Gross (she/her) is an MFA student at Western Kentucky University, having previously received a Master of Science in Information Sciences from the University of Tennessee. Though Brooke is studying creative nonfiction, she also has a passion for fiction and poetry. Her debut poetry collection, *Traitorous Muse*, is available on Amazon. When she's not reading or writing, Brooke can be found baking ugly but delicious desserts or planning unrealistic vacations. Find her on Instagram @btg3217.

Tyler R. Harris (she/her) is a blind pansexual woman living in Dundas, Ontario. She holds an undergrad and master's in history, and a master's in Poetry. She is working on her PhD in Poetry— writing a collection on disability joy, queerness, madness, and dating with low vision. Her poetry has appeared in Arc Poetry Magazine, Snowflake Magazine, Knee Brace Press, Skeleton

Flowers Press, and others. She has written a memoir, *Something Someday*, and a poetry collection, *Ragdoll*, both of which have yet to be published. She lives with her black cat Pugsley and dreams of being a forest witch. Find her on Instagram @tylersaurus1993.

Angela Heiser (she/her) lives near Raleigh. Her work appears or is forthcoming in *The Poetry Lighthouse, The Red Mud Review* and *County Lines*. Her poem "Cornhusker" was awarded the Poetry Genre Winner for the 2024-2025 issue of *The Red Mud Review*. She is an alum of Writers in Paradise and reads for Abode Press, Wildscape and Libre Lit. Find her on Instagram @angelacheiser.

Kedrianna G. Hiltonen (she/her) is an artist and poet from Georgia, US. She graduated from the University of North Carolina at Chapel Hill with a bachelor's degree in psychology. She is inspired by the destructive beauty of nature and humanity's cause and effect relationship with the Earth. She intends to explore the relationship with her writing and expand general consensus on the long-term effects of climate change. Find her on Instagram @grxffn.

Jackie Hollowell (she/her) is an extremely queer writer and the author of *Before the Flowers* (boats against the current). Her work has previously been published in Rogue Agent, The Dawn Review, and elsewhere. She has a love/hate relationship with capital letters and an all-hate relationship with capitalism. Originally from the Pacific Northwest, she now resides in Vietnam. Find her on Instagram (@6_hollowell) or on YouTube where she talks, mostly, about poetry.

Melanie Hyo-In Han (she/her) was born in Korea, raised in East Africa, and recently moved from the U.S. to the U.K. She is the author of *Abecedarian: Banff, Canada* (kith books), *My Dear Yeast* (Milk & Cake Press), and *Sandpaper Tongue, Parchment Lips* (Finishing Line Press), as well as the translator of several collections of Spanish poetry (Hebel Ediciones). Han has been awarded fellowships from Gladstone's Library, The Society of Authors, Sundress Academy, Banff Centre, and Casa Uno. She is the Co-Editor-in-Chief of *Flora Fiction* and the Two Languages Prize Editor at *Gasher Press*. Learn more about her at melaniehan.com and find her on Instagram @melhan.

Thomas Jackson (he/him) is a queer poet from Raleigh, North Carolina living with Bipolar Disorder. He is a published TEDx Speaker, landscape designer, self-published author, amputee, and suicide prevention leader. Find him on Instagram @jtommyj.

Claudia Jean (she/they) is a neurodivergent, disabled Filipino-German-American poet living in the Blue Ridge Mountains. She obtained her Bachelor's degree in English with classical training in creative writing, comic scripting, and editing. Her work focuses on identity as it relates to the body and spirit as separate entities and one cohesive self, using vivid imagery of nature and the divine to trace how generational trauma shapes both, inevitably determining the trajectory of our human condition. Also published for her poetry and memoir essays, Claudia's debut collection *The Secrets My Skirts Keep* was released in February 2024. Find her on Instagram @claudiajeanwrites.

alfonzo solomon kahlil (they/he) is a poet, playwright, and performance artist, raised on the W(b)estside of Chicago, who believes whatever doesn't kill you, makes for great art. Awarded Best Actor by New York Film Awards for their portrayal of Peter in *The Waiting Room* and Dramatist of *SCORPIO & THE NEW / NEW TESTAMENT,* alfonzo's art utilizes the spoken word as a medium to explore the realm of the profane, the profound, and the sacred of the interpersonal. alfonzo holds a BFA in theatre from New York University's Tisch School of the Arts and is represented by Stewart Talent. They were previously seen in *Measure of a Man (*Perceptions), *The Island* (Court u/s John), *HOLD UP, CANNABITCHES,* and *CHICAGO FIRE.* Find them on Instagram @alfonzokahlil.

Camille Lebel (she/her) is a mother to seven and lives on a hobby farm outside of Memphis. She's a Pushcart-nominated writer published in *Literary Mama, Sledgehammer Lit, Black Fox Literary Magazine, Inkwell, Last Leaves Literary Magazine,*

Writer's Resist, Thimble and more. She writes about child loss, evangelical deconstruction, and similar uplifting topics. Find her on Instagram @clebelwords.

Miriam Levy (they/them) is a queer artist from London working with poetry, performance and dance. Their creative work explores the relationship between personal and political, with a focus on care, community and rage. They enjoy language as a bold place with sharp edges, whilst also working with tenderness and expressions of love for queerness and queer people. They love prettiness and provocation. They have published poetry in several issues of t'ART Magazine, and non-fiction writing with Dansverkstæðið, Iceland. They have also performed poetry and movement together in live art, performance and gallery spaces. Find them on Instagram @miriam_levy_.

Sandra Beth Levy (she/her) is a retired psychologist who passionately practiced the healing art of psychotherapy for over forty years and is now pursuing her dream of immersion in creative writing and spoken word. She raised two biracial poet sons while honoring her Jewish-feminist identities. Her unique social and personal histories weave their way into her writing as she explores intricacies of love, loss, and the power of relationships as transformative agents. She has won local poetry slams and published poems with *Anomaly Poetry* and *Small Gems Press*. Find her on Instagram @slevy43.

Alecia Lewis (she/her) is a poet who worked her magic on stage and behind the scenes for various local theater groups. She participates in open mic nights throughout Louisiana. Her works have been published online on LSUA's 2023 and 2025 Verbatim websites and in print on the pages of Mythulu Magazine, as well as the Bayou Blues and Red Clay Poetry Anthology. She was January 2025's featured poet in the 318 Central digital magazine. She was crowned Poet Laureate in Poetry AEX's 2025 scavenger hunt. She is grateful and blessed for all the inspiration, guidance, and support that she receives. Find her on Instagram @neutralmuse73.

Elizabeth Mateer (she/her) is the author of the poetry collection *Searching for Home* (The Poetry Box, 2024). Her work has appeared in Beyond Words Literary Magazine, Radical Catalyst Art & Literary Journal and Four Tulips Press. Her second book, *A New Type of Breakfast*, is forthcoming in 2026 through Finishing Line Press. Additionally, she is an editor and Italian translator for The Poetry Lighthouse. She earned her BA in Creative Writing from Hunter College and holds a PhD in Clinical Psychology. Find her on Instagram @searchingforhomepoet

Homa Mojadidi (she/her) is an Afghan American poet and translator. Her translations and poems have been published in *Asymptote, Washington Square Review, One Art* magazine, *Beyond Words Literary* magazine, the *Blue Mountain Review*, IHRAF Publishes, and *Gulf Stream* (forthcoming). In her own poetry, Homa explores the themes of loss, exile, memory, and mysticism. Homa has an M.A. in English Literature from the University of North Florida and is pursuing an M.F.A. in Creative Writing with a concentration in poetry from George Mason University where she teaches creative writing and serves as the Poetry Editor for *So to Speak*. Find her on Instagram @homa_mojadidi.

Zoe Morana Liao (any pronouns) is a professional witch and podcast host of Magic Theory 101. She teaches classes on Taiwanese folk magic and astral projection. When not making people sob from deep spiritual revelation, she hosts dinner parties and does circus tricks. Find her on Instagram @zoemoranaliao

George Naranjo (he/him) is a poet, writing tutor, and student of the craft. Born in the Bronx, he developed an early love for storytelling and lyricism. Now based in Central Florida, he has grown alongside a diverse community of writers, continuing to hone his voice with the hope that his work might make even just one person feel understood. Find him on Instagram @naranjogeorge.

Allison Norwood (she/her) is a neurodivergent and queer poet born and raised in the Midwest. She has one previous poem accepted into an anthology that is not yet published and was an honorable mention for the 2025 Plentitudes Poetry Prize. She has been writing for over 20 years but only started sharing any of her writing last year. Find her on Instagram @springisbrutal.

Suzi Peter (she/her) is a Sudanese-American poet from Knoxville, Tennessee. Some of her other work has appeared in *Short Vine, Lodestar Lit,* and *The Mockingbird.* When she's not writing, she enjoys running, taking long walks, watching female-led films, and, of course, reading. Find her on Instagram @suzi_ptr.

Jessica Aure Pratt (she/her) is an occupational therapist who lives in Utah, where she enjoys camping and hiking with her family, and hanging out with her friends around a campfire or a maypole. Her poems often reflect experiences with parenting, nature, social issues, and many facets of spirituality. She is published in Wildscape Lit Journal, Moss Puppy Magazine, and Ink & Marrow. Find her on Instagram @jessaure.poetry.

Joshua Querijero (he/him) writes poetry in his free time when not doing schoolwork. He is currently a student at the University of Alberta. He has been writing poetry for a little over a year. He lives with his parents, brother and beloved golden retriever. Find him on Instagram @poemsbypogi.

Jay Rafferty (he/him) is a redhead, an uncle, an Irishman and an eejit. He is the author of three chapbooks, *Holy Things, Strange Magic & All That's Between Us is Time.* You can read his work in several journals including The Storms, Broken Spine Arts, FU Review Berlin and HOWL New Irish Writing. Find him on Instagram @simplyredinthehead.

Britt Reign (she/her) published her romance novels *Chokehold* in January 2024 and *BloodSport* in April 2025. Her first poetry book, *Will You Levitate*, was released in August 2024. She is also grateful to be featured in *Shadow Work Anthology* Volumes 1 and 2 with Grey Coven Publishing.

Brittany is a devoted dog mom, a physician assistant, and has a deep love for writing and traveling. Find her on Instagram @brittreignauthor.

Ash Reynolds (they/them) is a queer, nonbinary, ace poet living in College Park, MD, with their South African rescue mutt and 41 houseplants. They have been published in *new words {press}*, *The Bitchin' Kitsch*, and *Writers Resist*. Ash has poetry forthcoming in *Agapanthus Collective* and *Rogue Agent*. Find them on Instagram @ash.reynolds784.

Danielle Salerno (she/her) is a queer, ace poetess and Jersey Girl currently sweltering in Southwest Florida. Her work has been featured in *The Tongue is Sharp: An Anthology of Feminine Rage* and *Scenes of a Better World Zine*, and is forthcoming in the inaugural issue of *Prudence Dispatch* and Issue 2 of the *Azarão Lit Journal*. When her nose is not firmly planted in her notebook, she can be found singing with the Fort Myers Symphonic Mastersingers and chasing her loved ones around with a Tarot deck. Find her on Instagram @xfild.poetry.

Merrick Sloane (they/them) is a neuro-Queer 90's kid and nonbinary poet, editor, and researcher from Oklahoma who's a sucker for expletives and second languages. They hold an MFA in creative writing from the University of Tennessee, Knoxville and are Associate Poetry Editor of Doubleback Review. Merrick's work has appeared in *The Central Dissent: A Journal of Gender and Sexuality*, *Stories for the Road: Trauma and Internal Communication*, *BLEACH!*, *citizen trans* {project}*, and is forthcoming in *Puerto del Sol* and *ANMLY*. Merrick's poetry was recently selected as a winner of the Garden Party Collective's contest on Neurodivergence / Intersectionality and as a winner for AWP's 2025 Intro Journal Awards. Their work has received support from the DreamYard Rad(ical) Poetry Consortium and Sundress Publications. Merrick writes so that others may feel radically loved. Find them on Instagram @ontherunsince91_2.0.

D.A. Springer (he/him) is a writer, digital strategist, and the fire behind *Vision 2 Verse*, a creative sanctuary where transformation is both muse and mandate. With three powerful collections, *Virus Verses Vol. 1, Virus Verses Vol. 2*, and *Can't Stay Here: When Change is Destiny*, his work moves like prophecy: raw, rhythmic, and relentless in its pursuit of truth. Through a voice sharpened by experience and softened by grace, Springer crafts verse that speaks to the sacred chaos of becoming. Find him on Instagram @napalmjax.

Jillian Stacia (she/her) wants to live in a world where the coffee is bottomless and the sweatpants are mandatory. She spends her days crafting creative copy for clients in numerous industries and is known for her work in Children's Programming. Her poetry and creative nonfiction essays have been featured in Querencia Press, Plentitude Journal, Coffee & Crumbs, and Pile Press. Find her on Instagram @jillianstacia.

Rita Taste (she/her) is a bookworm who daydreams stories while running and always stops to smell the flowers. She is a fan of anything fantastical and morbid. Her writing inspiration comes from nature, traveling, and overcoming trauma. Rita's poems have been published in *Poetic Reveries, Glass Gates Publishing,*
and the nature anthology *Alchemy and Miracles*. Her short story, "Bloody Hungry" is published in *Funny Pearls*. When Rita isn't reading, she's watching anime with one of her two black cats on her lap. Find her on Instagram and BlueSky @littlebitespoetry.

Adeline Tatum (she/her) is a poet originally from Bayamón, Puerto Rico. She writes on themes of love, loss, and trauma. She grew up in a small town in Illinois and attended Kankakee Community College, pursuing a degree in Psychology. She was first published in the winter issue of *Sequoia Speaks* 2022 literary magazine and has been the co-author of a number of poetry anthologies, including *Because I F*cking Said So,* and *Harvest.* Her debut poetry collection, *A House With Bad Bones* was published in November 2024. Find her on Instagram @poetdreams16.

Waverly Vernon (they/she) is a writer and multidisciplinary artist currently studying at the School of the Art Institute of

Chicago, focusing on writing and ceramics. Their poetry has been featured in various publications, including *Chaos, Crises, Conflict* Anthology by Moonstone Arts Center (2025), where their poem "Flesh, Bone" was published, and *Wildscape. Literary Journal Mini Issue I*, which includes their piece "Alchemy of Her." Their writing navigates themes of identity, resilience, and the tensions of political and religious climates, treating poetry as both personal documentation and a tool for connection. What began as a private refuge has evolved into a bridge, linking shared and disparate experiences, and encouraging deeper engagement with the world. Find them on Instagram @anthologyofeleos.

Kassandra Vilchis (she/her) is a poet based in Minnesota. Her work thoughtfully examines themes of grief, womanhood, and generational relationships. Her writing appears in Bending Genres Journal, Rowayat, and the Upon Learning anthology. Outside of writing, she spends time with her dog, Thor and is dramatically lactose intolerant. Find her on Instagram @kassandra.vilchis.

Avril Shakira Villar (she/her) is a writer and youth leader from the Philippines. She is a mentee of the international organization WriteGirl LA. She won first place in the Poetry Competition by Beloved Summer Zine. Her poems are featured in printed books of RCC Muse and Arcana Poetry Press, alongside 21 poems, a song, and an essay published online in various international literary magazines. Find her on Instagram @shakira_soafer_latina.

Autumn Williams (she/her) is the author of two poetry books: her chapbook *Waves*, and her number one bestselling collection *Clouds on the Ground*. She's been featured in multiple publications and earned a finalist spot in The Wishing Shelf Book Awards. Her poems are influenced by the chronic illness she has, Myalgic Encephalomyelitis, but are written to be universal. Williams loves spending time with her husband and children, writing and reading poetry, and listening to music. Find her on Instagram @autumnwilliamspoetry.

Shui-yin Sharon Yam (she/they) is a diasporic Hongkonger living in Lexington, Kentucky. She is a Professor of Writing, Rhetoric, and Digital Studies at the University of Kentucky. She is the author of two books, *Inconvenient Strangers: Transnational Subjects and the Politics of Citizenship* (The Ohio State University Press, 2019) and *Doing Gender Justice: Queering Reproduction, Kin, and Care* (co-authored with Natalie Fixmer-Oraiz, Johns Hopkins University Press, 2025). Her writing has been published in outlets such as *The New York Times, Foreign Policy,* and *Hong Kong Free Press.* Find her on Instagram @yamsandchips.

www.ingramcontent.com/pod-product-compliance
Lightning Source LLC
Chambersburg PA
CBHW031523120626
46545CB00005B/1965